PROGRAMMER'S
GUIDE TO THE BRAIN

WITH EXAMPLES IN PYTHON

ROB VERMILLER

ISBN: 978-1-4834-0001-3 (sc)
ISBN: 978-1-4834-0000-6 (e)

Library of Congress Control Number: 2019909566

Lulu Publishing Services rev. date: 07/15/2019

CONTENTS

INTRODUCTION

Imagine we could program the brain. How cool would that be! We could lift our mood, raise our ambition, cure anxiety, bolster our self-confidence, improve our leadership skills, and alter our worst impulses. We could also create new, artificially intelligent companions and transfer our minds to powerful robot bodies.

So what's stopping us? First, we don't really know how the brain works. I believe our current understanding of brain function needs a fundamental revision. We can't program something we don't understand. Second, current theories of artificial intelligence (AI) and neural networks—based on our misunderstanding of the mind—are also cast into doubt.

I'm a computer scientist, not a neuroscientist or academic. But I know enough to say that AI—as currently conceived—is not how the brain works. So, in this book, I will intrepidly offer my own, perhaps fanciful, hopefully thought-provoking, alternative—something we can program.

So what's wrong with our current understanding of the brain?

We know the human brain contains around 100 billion neurons with many more supporting cells. Each neuron is connected to thousands of other neurons via synapses. Each neuron sends messages (electrical pulses) at a frequency up to 200 times per second to its direct neighbors. Scientists continue to devise clever lab experiments to study how human subjects think and behave. They poke and prod the brain and scan it using functional magnetic resonance imaging (fMRI) and other technologies to uncover its secrets (Le Bihan 2014).

Yet what have we learned? Do we know how memory works? No. Do we understand how traits like ambition, shyness, fear, or risk-taking are implemented in the brain? No. Do we know why happiness "feels" happy? No. Do we know why some people are narcissists or extroverts and others are not? No. Do we know the algorithms we use to identify a potential mate? What really happens in the brain of an ambitious person? How we make plans, learn faces, take risks, and experience awe? No, no, and no.

Instead, here's how a typical scientist describes the workings of the brain:

> The dopamine system is more or less obsessed with keeping us alive. It constantly scans the environment for new sources of food, shelter, mating opportunities, and other resources that will keep our DNA replicating … Dopamine yields not just desire but also domination. It gives us the ability to bend the environment and even other people to our will. (Lieberman and Long 2018)

I disagree. I think describing the brain in terms of molecules (e.g., neurotransmitters like dopamine) completely misses the point. A molecule is simply a bit of matter, a puff of smoke. It doesn't know anything about food, shelter, or mating. A molecule is not an algorithm or set of instructions. If we gaze at a picture of a serotonin molecule, do we get motivated? No. Are we visually stimulated at the sight of a hormone molecule such as testosterone or estrogen? Not in the least!

You can't program a molecule.

Molecules are simply messengers—smoke signals—helping to convey orders to an army of ready neurons in the brain. Like a general's command to charge, the signal itself conveys very little information. Much more interesting is how the receivers of the signal—the soldiers—are trained, what maneuvers they can perform, and the history and usage of their weapons. A general's order simply unleashes a complex process that's already in place. A molecule can't affect us unless our brains are prewired to be affected.

In addition to molecular explanations, neuroscientists also describe the brain in terms of its neural circuits and functional regions:

> Pride, shame, and guilt all activate similar neural circuits, including the dorsomedial prefrontal cortex, amygdala, insula, and the nucleus accumbens. Interestingly, pride is the most powerful of these emotions at triggering activity in these regions—except in the nucleus accumbens, where guilt and shame win out. This explains why it can be so appealing to heap guilt and shame on ourselves—they're activating the brain's reward center. (Korb 2015)

Again, I think this explanation misses the mark.

Yes, it's true that the brain is divided into specialized regions such as the prefrontal cortex, amygdala, and cerebellum. Planning seems to occur somewhere in the brain's frontal lobes. Emotion appears to bubble up from the amygdala, a specialized region consisting of around 12 million neurons. Short-term memory is enabled by the hippocampus. The brain stem is responsible for basic life functions and respiration. The cerebellum helps with coordinated motor control. The cortex—or gray matter—comprises around 20 percent of the brain's neurons and appears responsible for language, vision, and other higher-order capabilities.

But knowing which brain regions are more active when we engage in a specific activity doesn't help us understand how the mind is implemented. Describing the brain in terms of its gross anatomy and specialized regions is no more helpful than explaining it in terms of neurotransmitters and hormones.

You can't program a brain region.

Yet scientists continue to plunge ahead with their current approaches. The latest $100 million scientific research project called MICrONS (Cepelewicz 2016) endeavors to understand the brain by studying a cubic millimeter of a rat's brain tissue—containing 100,000 neurons and one billion synapses—in the visual cortex, the part of the brain involved in sight. Best of luck to them, but I'm not holding my breath. A similar $1.3 billion Human Brain Project, launched by the European Union in 2013, collapsed after only two years (Theil 2015).

To truly understand how the brain and AI work, I propose that we focus on the activity of individual neurons. They don't even have to be human neurons. The Open Worm project (openworm.org) studies a small nematode worm having only 300 neurons. Other scientists conduct research on large sea slugs—*Aplysia californica*—that have 20,000 central neurons in their nervous system, still a manageable number. Focusing on small worms and sea slugs is much more practical and has a much better chance of success in allowing us to understand how the brain works in general. Why? Because in small worms and sea slugs, many or all of the identified neurons have a unique function and carry out the same task across the species (Hoyle and Wiersma 1977).

Like sea slugs and nematodes, I speculate that human brains also contain identified neurons, each having a specific task to perform, although this is not scientifically proven. More radically, I think each neuron is responsible for the same function across the human species.

Think about it for a moment. If we all have the same set of identified neurons, it would explain a lot about how the brain works. Each neuron is accountable for performing a single, specific mental trait or task. Each neuron essentially becomes a computer on a network, able to run algorithms and programs, store information, and send messages to other neurons on the network. This is very similar to how the internet works today. Why not human brains?

Identified neurons give us something we can program!

When describing this theory of identified neurons, I'll deliberately ignore the influence of other, commonly ascribed causes for human traits such as genetics, epigenetics, neurotransmitters, and hormones. I believe a neuron-centric view can replace them all. Neurons bootstrap with programs and algorithms written in our ancestral DNA.

Any complete theory of the mind should also address where "feeling" and consciousness come from. I propose that the activity of individual neurons and their algorithms, in the context of powerful emergent effects, is the only explanation needed. The brain's simulation of reality, through the action of billions of individual neurons, begins to resonate in harmony, and "feeling" and consciousness are the result.

Many of these hypotheses may seem a little far-fetched, and in truth they are highly speculative and unproven. According to a critic:

> Here is what we are *not* born with: information, data, rules, software, knowledge, lexicons, representations, algorithms, programs, models, memories, images, processors, subroutines, encoders, decoders, symbols, or buffers—design elements that allow digital computers to behave somewhat intelligently. Not only are we not born with such things, we also don't develop them—ever. (R. Epstein 2016)

Clearly, I disagree. The ideas in this book are falsifiable, and that's how science advances (Popper 1959). Science is a way of thinking, not a source of absolute truth. Will these ideas ultimately prove to be correct? Perhaps yes, perhaps no. But I think anything is better than the current quagmire of our understanding.

Finally, I'll discuss the implications of this theory and how algorithms, trait diversity, and luck can answer persistent questions about free will, personal responsibility, and fairness. I'll address the social issues arising from AI and how we can best prepare society for the changes to come.

It's a lot to cover, so let's get started!

PART 1—IDENTIFIED NEURONS

AI Is Not How the Brain Works

Artificial intelligence (AI) is a hot topic these days, offering the promise of self-driving cars and trucks, automated factories, and world-class chess play. Yet the enthusiasm is also laced with foreboding: *Will a robot take my job?*

Current AI techniques are known by many names, including "neural networks" and "deep learning," a subset of machine learning (LeCun, Bengio and Hinton 2015). AI is used to mine big data sets to look for patterns, predict weather trends, diagnose complex diseases, monitor banking transactions for fraud, identify military targets, forecast stock market trends, convert speech to text, translate languages, enable factory quality control, understand handwriting, and—perhaps ominously—parse social media for consumer and political preferences.

AI can also be trained to recognize faces in photos and videos as we often see on TV police dramas. When a criminal culprit's face is caught on camera, it doesn't take long for law enforcement to identify him or her using AI facial recognition tools. AI is very good at finding patterns in big data, especially when millions or even billions of exemplars are available to train the neural network (Loy 2019).

1

However, as promising as AI might appear for these specific applications, dire warnings of an "AI winter" are mounting, as current approaches to AI don't explain how the brain actually works.

> To get a deep-learning system to recognize a hot dog, we might have to feed it 40 million pictures of hot dogs. To get [a girl] to recognize a hot dog, we show her a [single] hot dog …

> A computer that sees a picture of … doughnuts piled up on a table and captions it, automatically, as "a pile of doughnuts piled on a table" seems to understand the world; but when that same program sees a picture of a girl brushing her teeth and says "The boy is holding a baseball bat" we realize how thin that understanding really is …

> Self-driving cars can fail to navigate conditions they've never seen before. Machines have trouble parsing sentences that demand common-sense understanding of how the world works. (Somers 2017)

We're often willing to suspend our disbelief and accept that true AI and intelligent robots are right around the corner. We see them in the movies all the time, and they seem credible and real. But in reality, they are still a ways off.

NYU psychology and neuroscience professor Gary Marcus thinks AI—as currently conceived—is fragile, inflexible, and unable to generalize or think outside the box. AI can't think abstractly, make plans, or comprehend complex ideas (Marcus 2018a). Today, AI can merely recognize patterns. It can't currently do what humans achieve effortlessly. It lacks common sense. Neural networks are missing the innate prewiring required to learn.

One interviewer described Marcus's thinking:

> Say you wanted a machine to teach itself to recognize daisies … At first, the neural network is just guessing

blindly; it starts life a blank slate, more or less ... Given enough time and enough daisies, the neural net gets more accurate ...

But Marcus was never convinced. For him, the problem is the blank slate: It assumes that humans build their intelligence purely by observing the world around them, and that machines can too. But Marcus doesn't think that's how humans work. He walks the intellectual path laid down by Noam Chomsky, who argued that humans are born wired to learn, programmed to master language and interpret the physical world. (Thompson 2018)

We humans easily learn new concepts after a single example or exposure. We can generalize from a few examples. We effortlessly infer cause and effect. We pick up language quickly.

So how is the brain prewired to learn this way?

Scientists have long believed that human memories are stored in the connections, or synapses, between neurons in the brain. In 1949, Donald Hebb proposed that the connection weights between neurons are adjusted as we learn skills and remember new things. This process, known as "backpropagation," is "a procedure for rejiggering the strength of every connection in the network so as to fix the error for a given training example" (Somers 2017). It's the basis of today's AI and deep-learning artificial neural networks.

But recent research suggests other mechanisms at work. Our memories are not always stored in the connections between neurons but, instead, are stored within individual neurons themselves (Bédécarrats, et al. 2018). When scientists disrupted neural synapses in snail brains in a way that should have removed their memory of previously administered electric shocks, some memory remained.

In another experiment, when certain RNA molecules (similar to DNA) were transferred from the brain cells of trained snails to those of untrained snails, some of the trained snails' training (memory) was transferred too. This finding—that memories may be stored in RNA and are transferable—flies in the face of established theories that memories are stored via changes in connection strengths between neurons.

Taken together, these experiments don't offer a grand refutation of current brain theory and AI, but they do show chinks in the armor of the current paradigm. Although AI and neural networks offer powerful pattern recognition capabilities, they don't reflect how the brain actually works.

Since 2012, when it was used to win the prestigious ImageNet competition (Krizhevsky, Sutskever and Hinton 2017), the neural network approach to AI has become all the rage. But prior to that, AI researchers combined multiple techniques, including symbolic rule-engines, autonomous agents, simulation, statistics, and even Kalman filters (Russell and Norvig 2009).

Today, we're at an inflection point again, as researchers realize that neural networks are fragile, don't explain their decisions well, lack common sense, and require an overwhelming amount of labelled data to train them (Marcus 2018b). When the current paradigm begins to crumble, we need a new theory to replace it.

The brain is a complex adaptive system, with properties like unpredictability, non-periodic behavior, feedback loops, spontaneous order, adaptation and emergence (Holland 2006). To study how the brain actually works, I propose we return to earlier AI techniques, especially agent-based simulation (Abar, et al. 2017), whereby neurons are autonomous agents, and the mind emerges from their collective activity in a grand simulation of reality.

That's what I intend to demonstrate. Fancifully, of course!

Neurons as Little Computers

I propose that individual identified neurons are the primary actors (agents) in the brain. They each have their own unique agenda, and they zealously and relentlessly strive to achieve their goals and objectives. In the process, they cooperate and compete with other neurons in the brain for access to scarce bodily resources and attention.

Why do I propose this? For one thing, other complex networks—such as the public internet—take this distributed approach. Human society operates this way as well. The collective activity of each individual's self-interested behavior has unintended benefits—the "invisible hand" (Smith 1759)—that central planning could never equal.

In the brain, each of the 100 billion neurons is a specialized agent, an autonomous computer executing a unique program to carry out its assigned tasks. The most basic computer is called a Turing machine, described by Alan Turing in 1936. In its simplest form, all a computer needs to operate is a long tape (onto which it can write characters) and an interpreter which can process the current symbol (or instruction) on the tape. I speculate that each neuron is just such a computer. It's not a mainstream hypothesis, to be sure, but a few intrepid scientists have proposed that microtubules inside neurons can indeed support quantum computing (Hameroff and Penrose 2013).

A computer program processes inputs and delivers outputs. It repeatedly executes a set of instructions (loop), makes conditional assessments (if–then–else), and stores data (memory). That's what brain activity is mostly about, I propose.

A computer program is simply an algorithm:

> For many people, the word "algorithm" evokes the arcane and inscrutable machinations of big data … hardly a source of practical wisdom or guidance for human affairs. But an algorithm is just a finite sequence of steps used to solve a problem … Long before algorithms were ever used by machines, they were used by people …

> When we think about computers, we think about coldly mechanical, deterministic systems; machines applying rigid deductive logic … [However] tackling real world

5

tasks requires being comfortable with chance, trading off time with accuracy, and using approximations. As computers become better tuned to real-world problems, they provide not only algorithms that people can borrow for their own lives, but a better standard against which to compare human cognition itself. (Christian and Griffiths 2016)

In this book, I will de-emphasize artificial neural networks in favor of a more algorithmic approach, whereby neurons act as independent agents, running local programs in a massively distributed, resonating mind simulation. Although neural networks can also be considered algorithms, in some respects, I believe their black-box decision-making process remains too inscrutable for evolved traits. To the degree we humans employ machine learning and neural networks in the brain, I propose they execute within individual neurons themselves as helper functions.

So let's have a look at what the neural programming might look like.

Introduction to Neural Programming

The idea of a computer program running inside each of the 100 billion neurons in the brain might sound far-fetched. So take a deep breath, suspend your disbelief, and assume for a moment it's true. What are the implications?

Every program requires a programming language, a language of thought if you will. In neurons, the language must be ancient, written hundreds of thousands, or even millions, of years ago. Since we don't know what a neuron's programming language actually looks like, I'll use a modified version of the modern Python language in this book to illustrate the examples. (Python aficionados may protest some liberties I've taken with the language. I apologize in advance.)

Those with a computer programming background will know that most programming languages are essentially the same. They have subroutines or methods, variable assignments (A = 3), conditionals (if–then–else), arrays and lists (1, 2, 3, 4, 5), mathematical functions (A + B), and loops.

By my theory, each human trait is carried out by a single identified neuron in the brain. So let's assume there's a `SeekShelterNeuron` in the brain that's responsible for our behavior to find shelter when we're exposed to the elements like rain or snow. It seems like a reasonable hardwired behavior as we humans—and monkeys before us—have sought shelter throughout our history.

The neuron's programming—using a modern agent-based (object-oriented) style that encapsulates code into classes—might look something like this:

```
class SeekShelterNeuron:
    def ___init___(self):
        # Initialize the neuron once,
        # when it's first generated in the brain.
        self.exposed = False

    # Then automatically run this main routine at startup
    def run(self):
        # Repeat (or loop) the following code forever,
        # from birth to death of the neuron
        loop forever:
            # send a message to another neuron
            # to delegate a subtask or make a request
            # e.g., are we currently exposed to the elements?
            e = sendrequest("ExposedNeuron", "getstatus")
            # assign the resulting status to a variable
            self.exposed = e
            # then check whether the result is True or False
            if e == True:
                # The conditional statement (IF) is True, so
                # do something, e.g., move our legs and arms
                ... code not shown
            else:
                # otherwise do something else
                ... code not shown
            wait(clocktick) # wait a moment, rinse and repeat
        # Repeat the loop
```

The SeekShelterNeuron executes a unique program, which I've encapsulated into a class of the same name. (I'll assume there's only a single instance neuron per class; that's why I will treat classes and instances interchangeably for now.)

The class contains two methods or subroutines: ____init____ and run. The ____init____ method is executed only once, when the neuron is first generated in the brain, at or before birth. The run method then executes automatically after that. It usually contains a loop that repeatedly executes the code that follows it from the birth to the death of the neuron. In other words, every neuron in the brain is actively running a program all the time—none of this "we only use 10 percent of our brain" stuff.

A neuron may delegate subtasks to other neurons. In the previous example, a request or message is sent to the ExposedNeuron to determine our current state (e.g., whether we're currently exposed to the elements and needing shelter). [Narrowly-defined delegated subtasks like this may indeed employ local pattern matching and machine learning techniques.] A conditional (if–then–else) statement handles the two possibilities—True or False—likely by delegating additional subtasks to other neurons. The loop then waits briefly and restarts from the beginning.

To recap, the neural programming language supports the following operations:

- **Assignment of local variables** (using the [=] operator). In the example, the variable *e* is assigned a value: True or False.
- **Test for equality** (using the [==] operator). In the example, *e* is tested to see whether it equals True or False. "Not equal to" is denoted by the [!=] operator.
- **Conditional statements** (if–then–else). These allow the neuron to exhibit different behaviors depending on external or internal inputs or context.
- **Loops.** The "loop forever" statement endlessly repeats the execution of a block of code that follows it for the life of the neuron. In the example, a request is sent to the ExposedNeuron

every clock tick, waiting for a `True` reply. Most of the time, the neuron sits idly because we're not in an exposed situation (e.g., sitting in rain or cold). The neuron just keeps waiting—pinging—until events transpire.

- **Sending messages or requests.** A neuron can send a request to any other neuron in the brain using the `sendrequest` method. The destination or address of the message—that is, the neuron's name—is in quotation marks because the referenced neuron may be far away from the sender and may not even currently exist in the brain. Requests (and replies) take time to process and are routed from one neuron to the next until they reach their destination via other neurons that are already busy with their own tasks. Until the message is received, the reply is assumed to be `False`. Once received, it is locally cached.

- **Comments in the code.** These are preceded by a hash mark (#), and the program ignores them. Like a hastily written computer program, our DNA code is probably not commented very well for easy deciphering, but we can always hope!

I propose that this theory of identified neurons running code written (by evolution) in an agent-based (object-oriented) computer language, with integrated message passing between neurons, provides all we need to explain how the brain works. When billions of identified neurons simultaneously seek to carry out their own unique agendas, in cooperation and competition with other neurons, this massively parallel simulation begins to resonate with reality and takes on a life of its own.

The simulation aspect comes from how the neuron is programmed. After executing its short programming script, the neuron waits a clock tick, observes how the world has changed (via messages from other neurons), adjusts its internal state, then repeats the same script, over and over again, like a chess player repeatedly reacting to his opponent's moves, or an economist engaged in game theory. The mind emerges from this rich simulation of reality.

Loading the Program (from DNA)

For a neuron to act as a computer, it must first load its unique program. So where's the code? Why not in our shared human DNA library?

First a word about DNA, or "deoxyribonucleic acid." Each cell in the human body, including every neuron in the brain, contains a complete copy of the DNA library. The DNA library resembles a scroll—two meters long—containing 3 billion nucleic acids or "bases." [How a two-meter-long DNA molecule can be stuffed into each cell in the body is mind-boggling! But anyway, every neuron in the brain has access to the complete DNA library.]

There are four letters in the DNA alphabet—A, T, G, and C—represented by the four types of bases, adenine, thymine, guanine, and cytosine. This alphabet is comparable to the 26-letter English alphabet or the two-letter binary alphabet of 1's and 0's used in computers. It can represent concepts, words, and descriptions. And computer programs.

The DNA library contains 23 books or volumes (called chromosomes), onto which are written a total of 3 billion letters or characters, one letter per base. (Technically, we receive one set of chromosomes from our mother and another set from our father, so we have 46 chromosomes.)

Now a word about genes. All humans have the same 20,000 genes. Genes are books or chapters of the DNA library used to describe and express proteins and enzymes, which construct the body and control metabolism. (Technically, genes act as templates for constructing proteins. DNA bases are grouped into triples, or codons—ATT, GAC, and so on—which represent amino acids. ATG stands for methionine, TGG stands for tryptophan, and so on. Genes are thus translated into amino acid sequences, a.k.a. "proteins.")

Now the complication. Only 9 percent of our DNA is dedicated to genes (of which 2 percent acts as protein templates and another 7 percent is involved in gene regulation.) In other words, genes comprise only 9 percent of our DNA. So what does the other 91 percent of our non-protein-coding, non-gene DNA do?

Some scientists call it "junk DNA." I speculate that this junk DNA is actually a storage device for programs executed by neurons in the brain. Each neuron is assigned a unique section of junk DNA from which it loads and executes its program. In the rest of this book, I will ignore genes and genetics and will focus exclusively on the other 91 percent of junk DNA.

It's just a wild theory, but it does make sense. If neurons run ancient computer programs, then the programs have to be located somewhere. Why not in our collective human DNA? (To prove such a theory, perhaps a computer scientist can run a decompiler on our junk DNA to look for code fragments.)

Obviously, the neural code isn't written in English. It would be compiled into four-letter DNA-ese, similar to how modern computer code is compiled into a binary (base-2) alphabet. The programming code for each identified neuron is stored as a sequence of letters in one of the library books of our collective human DNA:

```
ATTGATCGGCAATGACTTAAGGGCACCGAT ... and so on
```

We humans are all 99.9 percent alike, DNA-speaking. We're so similar because at one point in our evolutionary history, as we left Africa, there were perhaps as few as 5,000 humans left on earth. Our DNA similarity has a stunning implication. If neurons load their programs from our collective human DNA library, it follows that we must all share the same neural programs! All humans have the same set of identified neurons running the same algorithms! It must be so because the 0.1 percent DNA difference among us is not enough to swap in and out different sections of DNA. We all share the same DNA.

DNA is a wormhole to the time of our ancestors. Millions of years of their experience is manifest in DNA, which transports that history to the present. DNA is time travel (Buonomano 2017). DNA is merely matter, but it's a different sort of matter than, say, a rock. A rock lives in the eternal present—a fleeting series of nows. It doesn't retain any memory of the past—lights, sounds, tastes, smells, touches, causes and effects. Over millions of years, we evolved from rocks, and water and gas, and life began to retain knowledge from the past. First, matter took on the shape of catalysts, which sped the rate of chemical reactions. Then, matter plus catalysts constructed more and more complex structures with feedback loops. Catalysts created more catalysts, along with more sophisticated structures like DNA, which began to replicate. More and more knowledge was manifest in the form of matter, and experience was retained and transported from the past to the present. Our neural programming—in our DNA—allows ancestral memories to resonate with present experience.

Not everyone agrees, however, that evolution can devise such elegant solutions as identified neurons and neural programs. Consider the following, for example:

> How genetics and development actually work, it's a mess. It consists entirely of hacks and patches all the way down. It's not modular. It's not agile. It's not anything that an engineer would recognize; it's just crap that runs. So when you go to try to reverse-engineer it, you can't. It's no good, because it was never engineered in the first place. So how do you devolve what has been evolved? That's like trying to unstir the coffee. (Veve 2018)

I disagree. Obviously humans can design things, and humans are merely a product of evolution. It follows that evolution can also design things. Indeed, intelligent design—and elegant solutions—may be an inherent function of evolution itself, or of any complex adaptive system.

Let me repeat that. Anything we humans can do—from setting up small Skunk Works labs (local innovation), to venture capital investment (scale-up), to radical redesign of current approaches (deployment)—can also be done by evolution because we can do it and we're simply a product of evolution.

Neurons Send Each Other Messages

A neuron doesn't have to do everything itself. It can delegate subtasks and solicit help from thousands of other neurons by sending them request messages. Those neurons can then delegate their sub-subtasks to other neurons, and so on. Pretty soon, the whole brain is lit up in a cascade of activity initiated by a single neuron. It's no wonder people think the brain operates holistically. The mind is the product of billions of individual neurons—self-interested and self-directed agents—each cooperating and competing for resources.

In the brain, each neuron is physically connected to "only" a few thousand other neurons. (The axon of one neuron directly connects to the dendrites of thousands of other neurons.) In order to send a request or message to one of its immediate neighbors, a neuron simply converts its request into a series of electrical pulses—like Morse code—and transmits the pulses via its axon wire to their dendrites.

The first time a `sendrequest` message is sent from one neuron to another, there will likely be no immediate response. The request will simply "time out," and the reply will be assumed to be `False`. However, after some time has elapsed, the asynchronous reply will eventually come back. Once it's received, it will be locally cached in the requesting neuron for better performance the next time it's needed.

Caching of results—like squirrels storing nuts for the winter—is critical to the operation of a massively parallel architecture like the brain. Even if the memory storage capability of the brain were infinite, we are limited by the time it takes to search for things and send messages to other neurons because of constraints on network bandwidth in the brain. It makes sense that neurons cache the results of messages into local working memory, inside the neuron itself, although that cache size is limited. Computer scientists have long debated the best strategy for cache management, including first in, first out (FIFO) and least recently used (LRU) (Christian and Griffiths 2016). It turns out that LRU is the most efficient way to manage the cache: message results that haven't been used in a while—like the stalest nuts in a squirrel's cache—are flushed from the local cache.

How can a neuron send a message to a distant neuron in the brain if the two are not physically connected? In computer science, there's a communication protocol called a "message passing interface" (MPI) whereby messages are sent to remote computers. Operating on a similar concept, neural messages could be routed from one neuron to the next until they reach their destination, either by point-to-point communication or broadcast messaging to many neurons simultaneously.

For example, on the public internet, packets of data are routed from one server to the next until they reach their destination. Likewise, each busy neuron in the brain—by this highly speculative theory—has a second job: to forward messages. To accomplish this complex task, each neuron maintains a "routing table" containing instructions on how to best route messages to remote nodes. (Routing tables can be built dynamically through trial and error by observing network traffic, or with the assistance of "routing protocols.")

```
class SomeNeuron:
    def ___init___(self):
        # initialize the message routing information
        self.routing _table = []
        self.immediate _neighbors = []

    def routerequest(self, requestor, reqtype, dest, params):
        # find the best routing for the message
        if dest == self:
            # process the request locally
            sendrequest(self, requestor, reqtype, params)
        else:
            rt = self.routing _table
            neighbors = self.immediate _neighbors
            via = determine _best _routing(dest, neighbors, rt)
            sendrequest(destination, reqtype, params, next=via)
```

The self.routing _table and self.immediate _neighbors are arrays of values stored in the neuron as local variables (i.e., local memory).

With routing, neurons can't expect to get an immediate reply to their sendrequest messages from other helper neurons and delegates.

Network latency may be an issue, and responses may lag, as anyone who plays games or streams content on the internet can tell you.

In this book, I'll assume that replies from other neurons arrive nearly instantaneously, but I realize this is an unrealistic expectation.

Neurons Have Unique Names

Aplysia californica are large sea slugs that graze underwater in tidal zones. When threatened, they release ink into the water to confuse their predators. Each slug has a tongue on its underside controlled by two neurons. When the slug is provoked, its siphon and gill can be quickly retracted (Moroz 2011).

Every aplysia has 20,000 central neurons in its nervous system. Many of the neurons are unique and carry out the same specialized function across the species.

Are we humans like sea slugs? Do we have unique identified neurons in our brain, each with its own task and identity? Do all humans have the same identified neurons?

Yes, that's my proposal, although it's a radical and as-yet-unproven theory. There's a single neuron in the human brain for, say, hunger, a single neuron that implements greed or ambition. Every neuron in the human brain has a specific purpose, a specific set of tasks—goals and objectives—to perform. The human mind emerges from the collective activity of individual, empowered neurons.

Why do I propose this? There are three primary reasons:

1. Evolution is lazy and conservative. If something is good enough for sea slugs, it's good enough for us humans. Evolution wouldn't reinvent the way the brain functions from earlier species unless there was a very good reason for doing so, and I don't think there is one.

2. Humans are defined by their evolved traits, fears, passions, interests, motivations, and drives. Does the brain implement each of these traits in a different way? Not likely. Evolution likely found a common approach for all of them. Identified neurons offer just such a powerful explanatory framework.
3. Neurons can't send messages to other neurons—for example, to delegate tasks—unless they know their name (or address) in advance, *a priori*.

This last point is crucial. Consider, again, the public internet. Each computer on the internet has a unique IP address that allows any other computer in the world to send it messages. Without a unique IP address, modern technologies like instant messaging, chat, and streaming video wouldn't be possible.

It's the same with neural communications. Each neuron must know, in its ancient programming, the name/address of every other neuron in the brain it wishes to correspond with. Without knowing, *a priori*, the names of all other neurons in the brain, there would be no way for one neuron to send a message to another neuron. (I'll discuss an exception to this rule in a moment.)

Using the proposed neural programming language described earlier, here's how a neuron might send a message to another neuron:

```
hunger_status = sendrequest("HungerNeuron", "detect")
```

In this example, the name of the `HungerNeuron` is known in advance by the ancient evolutionary code that references it. The task to determine (detect) whether we're hungry is delegated to this neuron by sending it a request. When the reply is received, it's stored in a local variable called `hunger_status`.

Because we humans all share 99.9 percent identical DNA, we must all share the same identified neurons. As new neurons are generated in the brain, they are assigned unique names from the DNA name directory. Once a neuron has a unique name, it bootstraps by loading and running its unique program, also located in the DNA library. That code then executes the neuron's agenda over and over, for a lifetime.

You may have spotted a flaw with the idea of uniquely naming each neuron. Cumulatively, our DNA is only 3 billion letters long. That's not enough DNA to store billions of unique names for each of the 100 billion neurons in the brain!

So let's modify the theory. Many neurons in the brain may be closely related clones. For example, the retina at the back of the eye contains millions of nearly identical neurons, each of them running the same program. Likewise, the visual cortex in the back of the brain, where visual processing takes place, also contains a large array of identical neurons. It's probable that each of these identical neurons is assigned a unique name algorithmically—for example, `RetinaNeuron-1234`—by adding a random number to the end of the neuron's class name when the neuron is generated. It can still be sent messages to its unique name/address, but as its name is not known until runtime (i.e., after birth), it must be registered upon generation by the `GenesisNeuron` if others are to be able to look it up.

Neurogenesis

After conception, the brain develops rapidly in the womb. Billions of new neurons are generated every day. Some scientist believe that process stops at birth, and we're born with all the neurons we'll ever receive (Sorrells, et al. 2018). But others have disputed this, contending that we continue to generate new neurons into old age, especially in the region of the brain known as the hippocampus (Boldrini 2018). I'll assume that either new neurons are generated into adulthood, or they are pre-generated (pre-allocated) earlier for later use.

New neurons are generated through a process called neurogenesis. Neurons connect physically—via dendrites and axons—to a few thousand of their nearest neighbors. That process establishes a basic physical network connectivity of the brain. Before neurons receive a unique name, they can

17

only send broadcast messages over the physical network. Once they receive a unique name (address), they can send narrowcast messages to each other.

If each mental trait is carried out by a single identified neuron, what happens when the neuron dies? Does it lose all its data and memories? Perhaps, as with modern data centers, each neuron periodically archives its memories to a remote storage device, likely a remote DNA backup tape. Then, when the neuron is regenerated (respawned), its memories can be restored by following a disaster recovery protocol.

Let's assume the existence of a single GenesisNeuron in the brain that acts as a factory to generate new neurons:

```
class GenesisNeuron:
    def ___init___(self):
        # start life with an empty list of new neurons
        self.neuron_list = []

    def sendrequest(self, requestor, reqtype, parameters):
        # this method responds to requests from other neurons
        # to generate a new neuron
        if reqtype == "generate":
            # generate a new neuron
            if parameters != False:
                neuron_class = parameters
            else:
                neuron_class = "GenericNeuron"
            new_neuron = New(neuron_class)
            self.neuron_list.append(new_neuron)
            return new_neuron
        elsif reqtype == "inventory":
            return self.neuron_list

    def run(self):
        # ensure all neurons listed in the DNA directory
        # exist, i.e., are generated or re-generated
        loop forever:
            directory = read_neuron_directory_from_DNA()
            loop for n in directory:
                e1 = sendrequest(n, "ping")
                wait(clocktick) # wait a moment
                e2 = sendrequest(n, "ping")
                if e1 == False and e2 == False:
```

```
            # The neuron didn't respond, so either
            # it doesn't exist yet, or it died.
            # [Disaster recovery protocol is not shown]
            # In either case, generate a new neuron
            sendrequest(self, "generate", n)
        wait(clocktick)
    # repeat loop
```

Neurons are generated either at the request of other neurons (perhaps to represent new concepts, as we'll see later) or automatically from the predefined DNA directory of neural names. Did I mention this is all highly speculative?

The `sendrequest` method of the `GenesisNeuron` processes requests to generate a new neuron. The new neuron is given a name prefix as an input parameter from the requester, or simply `GenericNeuron`. The newly created neuron is then added to the `self.neuron_list`, which can obviously get quite long.

Neurons listed in the innate DNA directory are automatically generated or regenerated by the `run` method. It continually loops through the predefined neural names in the directory and pings them to see if they exist. If not, it creates them.

(Python programmers might complain that there's no `New` function in the language to create an instance of an arbitrary class. But that's not what's actually happening here. The `New` function spins up a new computer—that is, each neuron gets its own virtual machine—gives it a unique name [e.g., `GenericNeuron-1234`], adds it to the network, loads its program from our shared DNA library, and starts the program running for a lifetime.)

There's One Neuron per Trait

Each human trait—desire, motivation, want, need, impulse, interest, or passion—is implemented by a single identified neuron in the brain. Each neuron runs its own unique computer program to realize its assigned trait. All humans have the same DNA, thus we all have the same set of identified neurons running the same programs. That's the basic hypothesis of this book.

Identified neurons are responsible for realizing specific traits in the brain: ambition, greed, shyness, compulsive gambling, and dominance, but also compassion. Each neuron is a highly focused and obsessed agent as it struggles to reach its goals and objectives and negotiate for shared bodily resources to achieve its ends.

It's not as crazy as it sounds. Having a single neuron per trait promotes better accountability inside the brain to ensure things get done. From an evolutionary perspective, identified neurons offer a practical solution for the mixing and matching of traits and the prototyping of new ones. The neuron bootstraps itself by loading its unique program from its local copy of our shared DNA, which manifests ancient wisdom from our evolutionary past: how to be ambitious, how to be hungry, and the like.

For example, let's assume a single HungerNeuron in the brain implements our need for food. The code would look something like this:

```
class HungerNeuron:
    def run(self):
        loop forever:
            s = sendrequest("StomachNeuron", "getstatus")
            if s == "empty":
                # do something
            wait(clocktick)
        # repeat loop
```

The HungerNeuron is responsible for compiling relevant information and providing a consolidated response. It delegates much of its work to helper neurons—in this case the StomachNeuron—by sending them commands or requests for information. These delegates, in turn, may then delegate their own subtasks. Pretty soon, thousands of other neurons become engaged like workers in a bureaucracy or a construction site, which lights up entire regions of the brain with activity, visible in PET scans.

Neurotransmitters as Network Optimizers

The search for food is an ancient and basic animal instinct. It evolved millions of years ago and was originally implemented using "old-fashioned" hormones and neurotransmitters. Ghrelin, for example, is a hormone secreted by the stomach when it's in an unstretched (empty) state, which triggers a brain hormone called neuropeptide Y, secreted by the hypothalamus.

This appears to violate a basic assumption of this book: that human traits and instincts are implemented by single identified neurons, not neurotransmitters, neuropeptides, or hormones.

I believe that as other traits—fears, motivations, drives, motivations, and so forth—evolved, it became inefficient (for evolution) to assign a unique molecule to each one. It's not easy to devise the complex biochemical pathways and enzymes required to manufacture each unique molecule.

The brain needed a more efficient and generalized mechanism to implement any of the dozens of traits and emotions. I propose that identified neurons provide the perfect elegant solution. Each trait is implemented by a single neuron that loads its programming from DNA—as all identified neurons do—and communicates via standard messages with other neurons to carry out its tasks.

So, what became of hormones, neurotransmitters, and neuropeptides? They're still there, of course, in the brain. But I believe that such molecules have been relegated to a relatively minor role. Now they simply serve to make the transmission of neural messages more efficient. Instead of having a neuron send individual messages to thousands of other neurons, broadcast messages can be sent via hormones and neurotransmitters. Like the general who shouts "charge!" to initiate a battle, it's more effective to send up a single smoke signal for distant troops to see and comply with, rather than communicate with each of them individually using messages.

In other words, molecules like serotonin, dopamine, testosterone, and estrogen are simply used for network optimization. Hormones and neurotransmitters don't cause happiness or depression or risk-taking or trust behaviors. They simply optimize the network of messages sent between neurons. Individual neurons have evolved to become the primary implementers of our traits and behaviors, and molecules now play a secondary and supporting role.

PART 2—MEMORY

The "iPad Neuron"

Some scientists believe a new neuron is generated in the brain every time we learn a new concept, even suggesting that a "grandmother neuron" exists in the brain (Bowers 2009). Since grandmothers have existed for millions of years of evolutionary history, it's certainly possible that the "grandmother" concept is itself innate.

But what about modern objects that didn't exist in the state of nature? How do they get into our brains? Take iPads for example. They weren't invented until recently, so there's little chance evolution has had time to incorporate that memory engram into our collective human DNA library. Is there an "iPad neuron" in the brain, and if so, how did it get there?

Let's take a step back. Why bother to remember an iPad at all? Because it interests us and motivates us, we crave it and covet it, and we envy our friends who own one. Without a strong emotion associated with an object, we simply can't remember it. We wouldn't want to remember it.

When we see another person gazing or staring intently at an iPad and then smiling, it triggers a feeling of envy in us toward the object. Bingo! Now it becomes meaningful to us. If we can associate an evolved emotion—for example, envy—to an object, then it's worth remembering:

```
class EnvyNeuron:
    def ___init___(self):
        # begin life with no objects of envy
        self.objects _of _envy = []

    def run(self):
        # The EnvyNeuron is constantly on the lookout
        # for new objects to be envious about
        loop forever:
            # Scan your "peripersonal space" i.e., the space
            # right in front of you, for people and objects
            x = sendrequest("PersonalSpaceNeuron", "getobject")
            p = sendrequest("PersonalSpaceNeuron", "getperson")
            if x != False and p != False:
                # OK, we see both a person and object
                # let's see if the person is gazing lovingly
                # at the object
                g = sendrequest(p, "gazing at", x)
                if g == True:
                    # OK, someone is gazing at a new object/pattern
                    # so append it to my list of things to feel
                    # envious about
                    self.objects _of _envy.append(n)
            wait(clocktick) # wait, then repeat the process
        # repeat loop
```

When the EnvyNeuron detects that another person is gazing at an object, it adds that object to our list of things to be remembered (i.e., objects of envy). Most of the hard work of perception—to detect whether someone is standing in front of us, in our peripersonal space, and then determine what they're gazing at—is delegated to other specialized neurons. Implicitly, the PersonalSpaceNeuron generates a new neuron to represent the sensory pattern of the object in front of us—the iPad—and names it something memorable like GenericNeuron-8675309.

The point is that we can't remember anything unless we can first associate it with an ancient evolved interest, drive, or emotion such as envy. Everything else, we essentially ignore. New object memories are attached to preexisting identified neurons to allow our evolved programs to find and interact with those neurons. An object of envy—represented by a newly generated neuron—only exists to us because it was added to our self.objects _ of __envy array. In other words, new memories remain closely associated with the original trait or emotion that made them worth remembering.

Through this process, the "iPad neuron" is generated. It then becomes the locus of all things iPad. It stores memories of all our iPad experiences and interactions. It has its own `run` method that's constantly on the lookout for iPads in our environment. It retains the original sensory pattern (transferred from the `PersonalSpaceNeuron`), and it constantly strives to learn all it can about iPads. That's its sole mission in life.

DNA Memory Storage

If objects and concepts that we perceive are represented by single neurons in the brain, how do they retain their detailed attributes? An iPad has qualities like shape, color, texture, and usage patterns. Where are these memories stored?

For decades, scientists believed that memories are stored between neurons in the brain as connections or synapses (Mayford, Siegelbaum and Kandel 2012). Such "holistic" storage is the basis of current artificial intelligence (AI)—so-called "deep-learning neural networks"—whereby connections between neurons are strengthened and weakened (using backpropagation algorithms) in order to learn and retain concepts and patterns.

But recent scientific discoveries have called this into question. It appears that memories may be stored within neurons themselves, not in the connections between them (Bédécarrats, et al. 2018).

We saw earlier that neural programs may be loaded from our shared DNA. It's possible that new memories are written back to DNA. "[S]ome have suggested that DNA ... is the most suitable candidate for memory" (Queenan 2017). Any new memories we form in our lifetime could be written to new strips of DNA held within individual neurons.

> The storage of information in readable symbolic form is not foreign to the conceptual framework of contemporary biologists. Both DNA and RNA carry information

forward in time, and there is elaborate machinery at the cellular level for reading that information. ...

[O]ur guess is that the answers ... lie at the level of molecular changes within neurons rather than at the level of synaptic changes within neural circuits. ... Among other things, this possibility increases the plausible density of information storage in the brain by many orders of magnitude. (Gallistel and Balsam 2014)

Let's assume for now that this is true, although it's certainly not yet scientifically proven.

DNA is a nearly limitless "disk" upon which neurons can store their memories. For example, in my digital music library, each of the thousands of songs—and millions of notes—on my playlist are somehow stored in my brain to sufficient fidelity that I can detect a single missing or dissonant note with ease. That's a lot of memory used, but I still have plenty of free space left.

DNA sequences can be used to store variables and programs and record new memories. When local variables are assigned in the neural programming language, local storage is dynamically allocated to store the value:

```
self.objects _of _envy = [] # list starts empty
self.objects _of _envy.append(n) # dynamically grow the list
```

DNA acts like a disk drive or memory chip onto which letters are written to represent almost anything. Whereas computers store memories in binary format (base-2) (e.g., 0110 1101 0001 011), DNA compiles memories into DNA-ese (base-4) (e.g., GATTACA ATTACAG). But all the formats—binary, DNA-ese, and English—are logically equivalent.

How are variables stored as DNA? First, the value is serialized into a string of DNA-ese characters: TGG CTT AGA CCT ... An array of pixels representing a high-resolution 1000 × 1000 image, for example, would be stored as a one-million-letter DNA-ese fragment (assuming that each pixel

26

is represented by a single DNA letter without JPEG-like compression). Short-term memories and long-term memories could thus be retained as strips of DNA recording tape inside a single neuron.

Memory (Brain) Transfer

Since we've established the principle that memories can be serialized and stored as DNA, it is not a stretch to assume that memories can also be moved around and transferred.

To transfer a memory, a neuron serializes it and transmits it via a message to another neuron located anywhere in the brain or body. Once received, the memory can be resaved locally as DNA. In other words, memories can be converted to electrical messages and then back to DNA.

Alternatively, memories could be transported by physically shipping DNA fragments from one neuron to the next. Recent research suggests that RNA can be transferred between cells (Haimovich, et al. 2017). This appears to be what happens in planarian flatworms, which can regrow their heads after they've been decapitated. Somehow, even after losing their entire brain, flatworms retain some past memories (Shomrat and Levin 2013). If memories can be temporarily stored elsewhere as DNA, then they can be retrieved through DNA exchange.

Memories can thus be passed around from one part of the brain to another, even from the left hemisphere of the brain to the right via the corpus callosum, a band of nerves that connects the two hemispheres.

But what about externally? Brain transfer has always been the stuff of science fiction. If only we could transfer our memories directly to other people—like a Vulcan mind meld—imagine the possibilities! Or, if we could transfer our memories to robots, we could live forever!

Perhaps ominously, our memories, experiences, and learnings could even be passed down to our children through DNA. No more need to warn them to look both ways before crossing the street or to refrain from texting while driving. They would be born with this knowledge.

Rob Vermiller

How would that work? If memories can be transferred from the brain (via messages) to neurons near our sex cells—sperm and eggs—then they could be manifest as DNA sequences and incorporated into our germinal DNA. In that way, our children could be born preprogrammed with our experiences. A little creepy, isn't it?

Ironically, the long-discredited theory of Lamarckian inheritance, whereby traits and memories acquired during our lifetime can be passed along to our offspring, is currently experiencing a resurgence in scientific interest (Balter 2000).

Here's how our memories and learned experiences could be passed along to our children via DNA:

```
class SexCellsNeuron:
    def sendrequest(self, requestor, reqtype, parameters):
        # handle a request from another neuron
        # to transfer its memories to our sex cells
        if reqtype == "memxfer":
            serialized_memory = parameters
            transfer2DNA(serialized_memory)
```

In this example, a memory—for example, how we evaded an enemy or what poisonous plants we avoided—is serialized and sent to the SexCellsNeuron for incorporation into our germinal (egg and sperm) DNA.

Certainly not all of our memories would be passed along to our children, only the "interesting" ones that aided in our survival. Perhaps if we observe a horrific war or famine in our lifetime, we can transfer that memory to our children to make them more wary and able to cope with the aftermath. Lamarck would be proud!

PART 3—BASIC MENTAL TASKS

Sense Perception

Every moment of every day we experience an onslaught of sensory experience. Visually, the human eye processes sixty frames per second in high resolution, with each image frame made up of millions of pixels (megapixels). It's a massive amount of data streaming into the retina at the back of the eye, much of which is conveyed to the visual cortex for additional processing.

Sounds enter the ear canal and vibrate the eardrum. The cochlea in the inner ear converts complex sounds into a set of discrete frequencies, accomplished by roughly 16,000 neuron-like hair cells that each detect a narrow frequency range (NIH 2014). (For those familiar with the mathematical concept of Fourier transforms, which identify component frequencies in complex sounds, the hair cells in the cochlea accomplish a similar task.)

Our senses convert raw experiences—sights, sounds, smells, tastes, touches—into neural messages and pass them along, semi-digested, to the cortex, the outer layer of the brain, which is two millimeters thick and gives the brain its unique folded appearance. The cortex comprises 20 percent of the brain's neurons, and specialized regions in the cortex called "cognitive maps" process sensory inputs. These cognitive maps are arranged into grids that represent the "feature space" of each sense.

For example, the auditory (sound) cortex is organized as a grid of tones. Neurons that represent closely related frequencies—pitch and loudness—are neighbors in the cognitive map. The visual cortex, by contrast, is organized by visual features like shapes, lines, and motions. Neurons that process our other senses—smell, touch, and taste—are also arranged into cognitive feature maps.

However, as discussed earlier, I don't think brain regions are important in themselves. Neurons are neurons. It doesn't matter in which region they live. Cognitive maps are simply a form of network optimization. If neurons frequently send messages back and forth, it makes sense that they would be co-located to prevent too much network traffic across the brain.

Our experiences arrive from the senses as a series of numbers or patterns. A complex sound, for example, is decomposed into its characteristic frequencies by the aforementioned hair cells in the inner ear and represented as array of numbers. We remember interesting sounds by storing the pattern of frequencies that make up the sound:

```
pattern = [246.94, 261.63, 277.18, 293.66, …]
```

However, the brain is not a general-purpose memory storage device. We only remember what interests us. All memories must be tied to an evolved interest—desire, passion, fear, motivation, emotion—otherwise we forget them. Important perceptions like a lover's scent or a predator's howl are committed to memory. Unimportant or commonplace inputs—like the fact that sun came up this morning, as it always does—are quickly forgotten. Events that failed to occur, like the sound of a train that always rattles by our window at two in the morning but for some reason didn't pass by last night, make us wake up and take notice. We remember expected but missing things as clearly as unexpected but real things.

Let's assume we hear a scream and then the sound of a predator's footsteps. This is the executable code:

```
class PredatorNeuron:
    def ___init___(self):
        # at birth, we've experienced no predators
        # so we begin life with an empty list
        self.predators = []

    def run(self):
        loop forever:
            s = sendrequest("ScreamNeuron", "detect")
            if s == True:
                wait(clocktick) # wait a moment
                p1 = sendrequest("AuditoryNeuron", "getpattern")
                if p1 != False:
                    # after we hear a scream,
                    # generate a new neuron to
                    # represent the sound
                    # of the predator's footsteps
                    n = sendrequest("GenesisNeuron", "generate")
                    # transfer sensory pattern to the new neuron
                    sendrequest(n, "transfer", p1)
                    if n not in self.predators:
                        self.predators.append(n)
            wait(clocktick)
        # repeat loop
```

What does this rather contrived example do? If we hear someone screaming and then we detect a strange rustling noise in the bushes, it's fair to associate the rustling noise with a potential predator lurking about. (Obviously the algorithm is much more complicated than this.)

In this example, the list of sensory "predator patterns"—sights, sounds, smells—that we know at birth is empty, a blank slate. However, this may not always be the case. It's likely we received some knowledge of predator patterns from our ancestors, predefined in our DNA library.

Again, a sensory pattern is merely an array of numbers. In the case of an auditory pattern, it's simply a list of numeric sound frequencies. To convert a sensory pattern into an object memory, the brain generates a new neuron—for example, a lion neuron or a tiger neuron—and then transfers the sensory pattern to it. The neuron is then added to the list of known predators.

From that day on, the new predator neuron constantly scans the environment, on the lookout for that specific pattern, and alerts other neurons if it detects a predator.

We All Perceive the World the Same Way

Philosophers have debated this question for millennia:

> Do we all see things the same way? … When I see a red apple, is the quality of my experience the same as yours? How could we tell? … Does the redness feel the same to me as it does to you? … The answer to the question … is very clearly "no." (Mitchell 2018)

I disagree. If we didn't all perceive the world the same way, we wouldn't be so troubled by the rare exceptions, like the word that some people hear as "yanny" and others as "laurel" (Salam and Victor 2018), or "the dress" that appears white/gold to some people and blue/black to others (Mahler 2015).

But more importantly, without shared perceptions, there would be no way for our innate traits and emotions to be associated with our shared experiences.

Here's an example:

In Newfoundland, Canada, moose sometimes stray onto busy roadways, especially at night, creating a hazard for oncoming motorists. To scare the moose away, vials of wolf urine are hung on nearby trees. Moose are born with an evolved fear of the scent of wolf urine, so it makes a powerful deterrent (Dockx 2017).

However, no wolves have existed in this area for generations. Moose there have never experienced a wolf. Therefore, the fear of wolves—or at least the fear of their urine—is evolved. Moose possess an innate memory of wolves—a sensory pattern of the scent of their urine—in their DNA, and this gets transferred to their brains.

Fear itself is obviously innate. Everyone experiences fear. But how can the object of fear be innate? How can all moose be born afraid of wolf urine?

There's only one way: all moose must perceive the scent of wolf urine the same way—that is, as the same sensory pattern or input. Otherwise, there would be no consistent target or object with which fear is associated in the shared DNA library across the species.

Every moose perceives the scent of wolf urine as the exact same sensory pattern. It must be so; otherwise, the following neural code that implements the fear of wolf urine wouldn't work:

```
scent_pattern = [29, 332, 118, 2, 937, 10]
if experienced_sensory_pattern == scent_pattern:
    sendrequest("FleeNeuron", "go")
```

All members of a species must perceive sensory inputs the same way—as the same characteristic and invariant number patterns. That's the job of the senses. Otherwise there would be no way to reliably compare modern sensory experiences with the ancestral patterns encoded in our DNA and then apply to them shared innate algorithms or trait dispositions once recognized.

Here's an additional example. Rats innately fear cats, specifically their smell. But a common parasite (*toxoplasma gondii*) is able to change rodents' behavior. Instead of fleeing a cat's odor, rats infected by the parasite are "mildly attracted to it" (Barford 2013). Cats then eat the docile rodents, and the parasite (which can only reproduce inside a cat's gut) lives on. This behavior modification would only be possible if the "fear of cats" instinct was highly modular, localized in the brain and easily exploited.

Our neural programming—in our shared human DNA—can have no common evolved reaction to what we perceive unless we all perceive things the same way.

Neural Networks as Pattern Recognizers

Today, there's a great deal of excitement about artificial intelligence (AI) and so-called "deep-learning neural networks." AI can beat human chess masters and even defeat experts at the game of Go. AI is behind self-driving cars, facial recognition, and intelligent factory robots.

However, this approach to AI is not new. It's based on thirty-year-old technology called "backpropagation" that's used to train artificial neural networks. Deep learning offers a way to train multiple layers of "artificial neurons"—resembling a neuron sandwich, whereby every neuron in one layer is connected to every neuron in the next layer—to recognize patterns.

The first layer of the network, consisting of input or "sensory" units, receives information from the outside world. The final layer, consisting of output or "reporting" units, responds according to what it has learned from the inputs. The intervening or hidden layers of neurons store the learnings as variable weights assigned to the connections between units.

For example, the input units can be shown a photo of a human face. In this case, there are millions of input units, each corresponding to a pixel in the image. Each input unit is connected to all units in the next layer of the network, which are in turn connected to the next (hidden) layer, and so on, until the final output layer. The connection weightings in the hidden layers are each initially assigned a random value.

We can ask the output units to identify whether a specific person is in the image. The output units initially provide responses that are no better than chance.

Training of the network is achieved by adjusting the weights of all the neural connections in all layers using backpropagation to reduce the output prediction error. All connections in the network that contributed to the correct answer are strengthened, and connections that didn't have their weights weakened to reduce the difference (error) between the actual output and the correct output.

After undergoing thousands or millions of training events—that is, looking at different labeled photos—the neural network gets quite good at discerning patterns.

And that's the problem. For neural networks to generalize well, they must be fed millions of examples to minutely adjust all the connection weights between neuron units. A nine-layer neural network with 60 million parameters and 650,000 neurons must be trained using 1.2 million distinct examples (Krizhevsky, Sutskever and Hinton 2017).

Obviously, the human brain doesn't work this way. A child can learn a new word after hearing it once, without undergoing this repetitive training process.

Artificial neural networks are unable to truly generalize, think abstractly, or make plans. They don't implement the if–then–else conditionals or loops or the variable assignments found in algorithms. They can only recognize patterns. They lack common sense. Modern AI—deep-learning artificial neural networks—can't be considered a general solution to artificial intelligence (Marcus 2018a).

Perhaps, though, the brain employs something resembling neural networks for specific narrow purposes such as basic pattern recognition. Connection weights from the trained model can even be stored as an array of numbers in our ancestral DNA and used for pattern recognition. Recent discoveries about "reward prediction error" circuits in the brain offer a clue on how this might work, perhaps using dopamine as a mechanism (Lieberman and Long 2018).

But generally, neural networks don't mimic how we plan or how we think. Those capabilities, I believe, are agent-based (object-oriented) and algorithmic, and bootstrapped from our DNA.

Organic Motion

Ragdoll physics is fun to watch and play with. In a computer game or app, for example, we can interact with a simulated human body, pick it up and drop it, see it fly through the air, shoot at it, and even observe it as it collides with other objects. It's strangely addictive. See here for an example: https://schteppe.github.io/p2.js/demos/ragdoll.html (Hedman).

In ragdoll physics, every solid object—arm, leg, torso, head—has mass and spring-like connections to other objects via joints and tendons that serve to constrain and dampen their movement. Muscles resist the pull of gravity and make the body move.

A so-called "physics engine" inside modern 3-D computer games maintains a list of each object along with its physical properties (mass and velocity) and connections (e.g., arm connects to torso). Then, for an extremely short period of time (clocktick), the engine computes all the forces, including gravity, acting on each object and determines which direction it will go next. (If you want more details on how a physics engine works, follow the URL above and examine the JavaScript code.)

Modern computer games such as Fortnite are good at keeping their characters in constant organic motion to make them look more real and alive. When we see such organic forms, our reaction is immediate and hardwired. We recognize them as living creatures in the way they bob and weave in subtle ways around us. We compare our prediction of their motion to their actual motion, and any prediction error leads to surprise, as follows:

```
class OrganicMotionDetectorNeuron:
    def run(self):
        loop forever:
            # Detect objects in peripersonal space
            # i.e., nearby, within arm's reach
            objects = sendrequest("PersonalSpaceNeuron","getobjs")
            joints = sendrequest("PersonalSpaceNeuron","getjoints")
            loop for obj in objects:
                … insert physics engine prediction code here
                if actual _location != predicted _location:
                    # object not in organic motion
                    sendrequest("DistressNeuron", "go")
            wait(clocktick) # wait, then repeat
        # repeat loop
```

Even babies utilize a naive form of physics to detect and confirm organic shapes in their environment. Organic shapes are appealing and warm. If an adult remains motionless like a statue, babies feel distress and cry (Bloom 2013). Our caregivers wouldn't be recognizable—in fact, they may even be a little disturbing and creepy—if they weren't in constant organic motion.

Object Recognition

The ability to recognize objects comes so naturally and intuitively to us that we forget to appreciate the underlying complexity. We receive a grainy stream of images from our eyes. Objects are partly occluded or hidden by shadows, yet somehow the retina and visual cortex can extract features from this mass of messy data.

We can visually track objects based on their continuity in space and time, not necessarily by their other features like color (Carey 2009). Even infants develop an understanding that unsupported objects fall and that an object that is briefly covered by another object or a curtain doesn't cease to exist. Objects remain in our mental simulation even when we can't see them.

Objects are in constant motion relative to our eyes. We use that information to identify object boundaries, paths, and spatial relations. Our two eyes are set apart, and the slightly different images perceived by each eye can be overlaid to create a 3D representation. The fourth dimension—time—is used to measure distance. The longer it takes us to walk to an object, the farther away it is.

Programming an object recognizer and tracker is highly complex and outside the scope of this book. Many open-source projects, such as OpenCV, have made sophisticated computer vision algorithms available to implement such object tracking (Solem 2012). Give them a try!

Stereotyped Behavior

An albatross is a large seabird with a wingspan of up to twelve feet that lives mostly in the Southern Hemisphere. Amazingly, it can fly nearly

10,000 miles in a single journey and circumnavigate the globe in 46 days by riding wind currents.

When it settles down to mate, the albatross relies on a set of stereotyped instincts and behaviors, including dancing, staring, and preening. The albatross mates for life and always comes back to the same location to nest.

For an albatross, egg laying and chick rearing also involve highly ritualistic behavior. Albatrosses lay only a single large egg—between 7 and 18 ounces in weight—per breeding season. Both parents help incubate the egg in multiweek stints. The incubation period lasts around 75 days, the longest of any bird, and it can take over a year to raise a chick.

However, the albatross's evolved behaviors are remarkably fragile. The albatross has only a single instinctual (stereotyped) motion for gathering the egg or material for its nest. If the egg rolls away from underneath it, it will not retrieve the egg. It lacks a mental model, or common sense, in terms of understanding that eggs can roll away and where they may roll to. The albatross simply gives up without trying.

Statistically, if all albatrosses in the flock apply these simple stereotyped behaviors to care for their eggs, enough eggs will make it through incubation for survival of the species, even though individual albatrosses may be out of luck. For the albatross, common sense was deemed overkill by evolution.

Let's assume the stereotyped egg-gathering instinct is implemented by a single neuron in the albatross brain. The code would look something like this:

```
class GatherEggNeuron:
    def run(self):
        loop forever:
            context = sendrequest("ContextNeuron", "getvalue")
            if context == "sitting on egg":
                egg = sendrequest("EggNeuron", "detect")
                if egg == False:
                    sendrequest("GatheringMotionNeuron", "go")
            wait(clocktick)
        # repeat loop
```

The albatross's `GatherEggNeuron` constantly pings the `ContextNeuron` to determine whether it detects that the bird is currently sitting on an egg. If so, it verifies with the `EggNeuron`—which represents the egg concept in the brain—that the egg is still there (detected). If not, it initiates the stereotyped gathering motion via the `GatheringMotionNeuron`.

Unfortunately, the egg neuron has no sophisticated model of where the egg may have rolled. If the egg is gone and the stereotyped gathering motion doesn't work, the bird is free to get up, walk away, and do other things.

Does the albatross feel sad or empty if it loses the egg? Perhaps. Its entire brain simulation of reality must abruptly reconfigure itself from one context to another. That is loss.

Fight or Flight

When threatened by a predator or criminal, our fight-or-flight response is triggered. We either stand our ground and fight or turn our back and run.

```
class FightOrFlightNeuron:
    def ____init ____(self):
        # Assume we're not terribly brave
        self.bravery __level = 0

    def run(self):
        loop forever:
            threat = sendrequest("ThreatNeuron", "detect")
            if t != False:
             if self.bravery __level < 50:
                 sendrequest("WalkOrRunNeuron", "awayfrom", threat)
            wait(clocktick)
        # repeat loop
```

If we detect a threat, we may run away (or not), depending on how brave (or stupid) we are. In the previous example, it is assumed that we're born with a fixed and predetermined `bravery __level = 0`. (Later we'll explore how inborn traits can have variability.)

Learning to Walk

The `FightOrFlightNeuron` assumes the existence of a `WalkOrRunNeuron`. But how can it assume that? Babies certainly can't run. Running and walking are learned abilities. How can an evolved instinct refer to a learned skill that doesn't exist until later?

In computer science, there's a concept known as "late binding." We can refer to things that don't yet exist if we're confident they will exist later. Running is a learned skill, but it's one we can usually depend on to develop.

Evolution was certain that a `WalkOrRunNeuron` would exist because it put it there. The neuron was likely generated (in an untrained state) before birth, and evolution gave it the code to motivate the subject to learn to walk and run. After the learned skill is acquired, any other neuron can send it requests to leverage that learned ability.

In other words, an evolved instinct implemented by the `FightOrFlightNeuron` already knows the name, *a priori*, of the learned skill—implemented by the `WalkOrRunNeuron`—before that skill exists, so it can reference it in its ancient code.

How can the `WalkOrRunNeuron` train itself to walk when it knows nothing about walking? Philosophers have debated this question for centuries. Plato asked in his dialogue *Meno* how we can begin to learn anything if we have no notion about what is to be learned or how to recognize that, indeed, we have learned something new. Not knowing about DNA or evolution, he suggested that the human soul already has knowledge of everything. Later, French philosopher and mathematician René Descartes proposed the rationalist doctrine that ideas are innate. This, in turn, provoked fierce opposition from philosopher and physician John Locke, who believed that the mind at birth is a "tabula rasa" or blank slate and that everything we know is learned from experience. The philosopher Immanuel Kant felt otherwise, however, when he declared the obvious: we can only sense things for which we were built, and there are limits to what we can perceive.

Clearly, Locke was wrong; we're not born as blank slates. We can't learn to walk without predefined programming—in our DNA—to provide the motivation and guidelines for our learning process.

It seems a contradiction that learned abilities are innate, but it's a common pattern in nature. Songbirds such as zebra finches have two evolved brain modules involved in their singing. The first module describes roughly how to sing, and the second enables the birds to correct their mistakes through experience, perhaps by listening to other birds.

Our DNA contains neural programming to establish the ability to walk and run. That programming doesn't know exactly what those skills will look like, but it knows roughly what it takes to learn them. For example:

```
class WalkOrRunNeuron:
    def ___init___(self):
        # start life without the ability to walk or run
        self.walking = []
        self.walking_ability = False

    def sendrequest(self, requestor, reqtype, parameters):
        # reply to queries from other neurons
        # asking if we can walk or run yet
        if reqtype == "is trained":
            return self.walking_ability

    def run(self):
    loop forever:
        if self.walking_ability == False:
            # Can't walk yet. Enter training mode.
            # Look for a handhold in your peripersonal
            # or nearby space
            h = sendrequest("PersonalSpaceNeuron", "handhold")
            if h != False:
                sendrequest("HandNeuron","grab and pull up", h)
                b = sendrequest("BalanceNeuron", "getpattern")
                l = sendrequest("LegNeuron", "getpattern")
                n = sendrequest("GenesisNeuron", "generate")
                # transfer the balance and leg motion pattern
                # to the new neuron
                sendrequest(n, "transfer", (b, l))
                self.walking.append(n)
        wait(clocktick)
```

41

Rob Vermiller

If we can't yet walk, we begin the training process: we grab any handhold in our peripersonal (nearby) space and try to pull ourselves up. Our legs move to compensate for lost balance, and the resulting changes to balance and leg movement patterns—a primitive form of walking—are retained as muscle memory.

There are hundreds of thousands of muscle fibers in the leg, each controlled by neurons. Patterns are an array of signals (numbers) a neuron sends to each individual muscle fiber, indicating when it should contract in precise sequence over time. After training, the pattern is played back to enact the skill of walking or running.

Babies learning to walk will first appear jerky and uncoordinated. Later, as they gain skills, their movements become more graceful, likely using something akin to a deep learning neural network to train the subtleties. Movement involves a highly choreographed dance of muscles, bones, and tendons, as well as feedback from the senses—touch and sight—to provide guidance. Nerves embedded in our muscles provide confirmation of extension and movement.

Eventually, the skill becomes an unimaginably complex series of patterns, observations, feedback loops, and error corrections, all stored as numeric arrays. But the overall learned skill is controlled by a single `WalkOrRunNeuron`. Having a single pre-identified neuron accountable for each skill allows these skills to be exploited by our ancient programming.

Learning Faces

Philosophers from Jean-Paul Sartre to Michel Foucault have reflected on "the look" or "the gaze"—the act of seeing and being seen. We're like monkeys, using our stare to establish power relations over others. "Hell is other people," admitted Sartre.

We broadcast our emotions through facial expressions as anyone around us can tell. We easily detect another person's joy, fear, disgust, anger, sadness, and surprise. When we're sad, we furrow our brow and make our eyes appear smaller. When we're happy, we raise our eyebrows and make

42

our eyes look bigger. Others see our expressions and react with empathy, shared happiness, or fear. The eyes are the window to the soul, or at least to our emotions and intentions.

We're born with an innate capacity to learn and recognize faces and their emotions:

> There is an innate representation of what human faces look like—an innate face schema—that clearly plays a role in recognizing faces as such, learning to identify one's mother's face, identifying eyes and the focus of gaze, and supporting facial imitation.

> We know that even newborn infants have representations of faces; they preferentially attend to faces over other stimuli of comparable complexity and they imitate facial gestures of others, producing the same gestures themselves. (Carey 2009)

The basic facial pattern consists of two smaller circles—eyes—residing at the center line of a larger circle, the face. Any caricature portraitist knows the exact ratios and relative position of the ears, nose, and mouth.

Computers can classify faces and emotions according to the Facial Action Coding System, or FACS. Indeed, at least half of US adults have been entered into face recognition databases, such as the FBI's Facial Analysis, Comparison, and Evaluation (FACE), which uses photo sources like driver's licenses and mug shots. Computer algorithms pick out facial features like the distance between the eyes or the shape of the chin, and this "face template" is compared to data from the other faces collected. The system returns a list of possible matches, ranked by probability score of correct identification. Better lighting, image resolution, and view angle improve the probability of a match.

At Facebook, the DeepFace (deep-learning facial recognition) system can identify human faces in digital images with 97 percent accuracy and automatically suggest friends to tag in photos. The system was trained on 4 million images uploaded by Facebook users. DeepFace successfully employs a nine-layer neural net with over 120 million connection weights. In theory, we could post a picture of anyone in the world and have Facebook instantly identify who is in the photo: a law enforcement officer's dream or a privacy advocate's nightmare!

For humans, facial recognition appears effortless. We easily locate friends in crowds, and children enjoy the challenge of a "Where's Waldo?" game. However, once we lose the specialized neurons involved in facial processing—through stroke, or injury, or DNA mutation—we experience a condition known as face blindness or agnosia. *Alexithymia* is the term for people who have difficulty identifying and describing emotions on other people's faces, often associated with autism. Such specificity in cognitive processing—a mild and localized stroke can wipe out an entire human capability—lends credence to the identified neuron hypothesis, whereby single neurons are responsible for complex human abilities.

So let's assume facial recognition in the brain is accomplished by a single neuron:

```
class FaceNeuron:
    def ____init____(self):
        # start life with an empty list of faces
        # that we can recognize
        self.faces = []

    def run(self):
        loop forever:
            pattern = sendrequest("FacePatternNeuron", "detect")
            if pattern != False:
                n = sendrequest("GenesisNeuron", "generate")
                # transfer the pattern to the new neuron
                sendrequest(n, "transfer", pattern)
                if n not in self.faces:
                    self.faces.append(n)
            wait(clocktick)
        # repeat loop
```

The FaceNeuron constantly scans the visual field for face-like patterns. Facial recognition itself is an example of pattern matching delegated to the

`FacePatternNeuron`, perhaps using AI techniques like deep-learning neural networks. Face trackers have been popularized by Snapchat filters and augmented reality (AR) applications like Pokémon GO that have brought the technology into the mainstream, although the underlying algorithm is too complex to explore here.

Once a face is detected, assuming we've never seen the face before, we retain the face pattern memory in a newly generated neuron. For example, the first time we see the actress Jennifer Aniston, we generate a `JenniferAnistonNeuron` (Quiroga, et al. 2005). The mission of the new neuron is to identify her in a crowd (in magazines, on TV shows, etc.) and retain the memory of any new information or gossip about her.

Agency, or "He Did It"

Human agency involves understanding the goals and intentions of other people (agents). What are they thinking? What are they trying to do? What do they believe?

Even children understand the actions of others as goal-directed; that is, they know there must be a purpose behind what others are doing: are people trying to manipulate us, or can we manipulate them?

Again, understanding the intentions of others often begins with the eyes:

> Gaze following … requires representations that identify
> eyes, such that a shift in direction of the eyes may trigger
> the child's shift in attention in the same direction. (Carey
> 2009)

We follow the gaze of others to identify what objects they're interested in, and then we remember their beliefs, goals, and intentions. Here's what the code might look like:

```
class AgencyNeuron:
    def ____init____(self):
        # begin life with an empty list of agents
        self.agents = []
```

```
def run(self):
    loop forever:
        # look for people and objects in your
        # peripersonal (nearby) space
        x = sendrequest("PersonalSpaceNeuron", "getobject")
        p = sendrequest("PersonalSpaceNeuron", "getperson")
        if p != False and x != False:
            # OK, we see both a person and object
            g = sendrequest(p, "gazing at", x)
            if g == True:
                # What is the intent or purpose of their gaze?
                … code not shown
        wait(clocktick)
    # repeat loop
```

We observe someone staring or gazing at an object, perhaps a baseball bat. What do they plan to do with it? Go out and play, or hit us over the head?

It's an important survival skill to ascertain the motives, beliefs, and intentions of others. We apply an innate model or set of rules learned through millions of years of evolutionary history to uncover hidden motives in others, for example:

- If we know the person well—perhaps it's a family member—then we can assume the best, that their intentions are likely benign and honorable, even friendly.
- If we don't know the person well or if they have a bad reputation, then we assume the worst.
- If we know the person well but recently had a fight with them—or if they're unstable—then we should remain vigilant.

We generate a new neuron in the brain to represent each person we meet. We need a place—a filing cabinet—to retain everything we know about that person for later assessments. (We're probably optimized to track up to 150 individuals closely as that was the number of people in hunter-gatherer groups when we last evolved.)

Defining the rest of the algorithm—to determine another person's intentions—is left as an exercise for the reader.

PART 4—WHY DO I "FEEL"?

Emotions

Without emotions—and motivations, interests, fears, desires, passions, and so on—we'd never get out of bed in the morning. We'd simply cover our head with the pillow and go back to sleep. The naturalist Charles Darwin suggested that emotions are evolved traits that aid in our survival as a species (Darwin 1872). We're all born with a finite set of emotions, and it's hard to imagine what a new emotion might even look like.

Generally, emotions fall into one of eight universal categories, meaning that they're shared across all members of the human species (Plutchik 2003):

1. happiness, joy
2. fear, anger, rage
3. sadness, grief
4. disgust, contempt
5. surprise, shock, amusement, excitement
6. shame, embarrassment, guilt, loneliness
7. pride in achievement, relief, satisfaction
8. envy, jealousy, pity, indignation

According to my theory, each emotion is implemented by a single identified neuron—having a unique program, loaded from our DNA—in the brain.

Using this approach, we shouldn't find it hard to invent an entirely new emotion from scratch. Here's an assignment for extra credit:

> Write the code for the `AechiaNeuron` that implements a new emotion called "aechia" that is a "gipsa" of *asteroids*. (Hint: Start with an existing pattern like social anxiety, which is a fear of social situations.) Maybe gipsa is an attraction, or maybe it's a repulsion, or maybe it's an obsession with asteroids.

Apart from the "feeling" itself, an emotion is just an algorithm.

"Feeling"

Qualia or "feeling" is the subjective experience of pain, pleasure, happiness, sadness, and so forth. But scientists don't really know why we "feel" or how "feelings" arise in the brain:

> It is the tune stuck in our head, the sweetness of chocolate mousse, the throbbing pain of a toothache, the fierce love for our child and the bitter knowledge that eventually all feelings will end.
>
> The origin and nature of these experiences, sometimes referred to as qualia, have been a mystery from the earliest days of antiquity right up to the present …
>
> What must happen in our brain for us to experience a toothache, for example? Must some nerve cells vibrate at some magical frequency? …
>
> The truth is that we do not know. (Koch 2018)

So let me offer my own answer (stick with me; I'll try not to get too metaphysical). I believe "feeling" arises from perturbations of the mind. Let me explain.

I believe that the mind is a grand simulation that remains highly synchronized with, but separate from, reality. In that simulation, we are free to navigate backward and forward in time and space, recall the past, and plan for the future, with an independent, movable perspective. The mind is literally a parallel universe, a simulation of objects and causality and relationships in the real world. The parallel universe allows for perception, prediction, consideration of alternate scenarios and perspectives, and understanding of cause-and-effect.

"Feeling" arises from fluctuations and perturbations in the mind's simulation or parallel universe. When we "feel" happy, it corresponds to an opening up of new possibilities in the simulation. When we "feel" shame or guilt, certain areas of the simulation become off-limits, shut down, or appear off-line. With shame, for example, we simply can't lift our eyes to face a screaming parent, no matter how hard we try. Our freedom is restricted, and that restriction is "feeling". It's nothing more than that.

The goal of the mind is not happiness, as the philosopher Aristotle believed, but harmony and resonance with reality. Resonance is how the brain achieves transcendence from mere matter such as rocks and water. Resonance happens when one object vibrates in sympathy with another object. As an analogy, when we play an E or an A on a violin, the strings on nearby violins begin to vibrate sympathetically at the same frequency and echo the same note, like a tuning fork. Dissonance, on the other hand, creates "feeling".

In the brain, each neuron sends signals to other neurons 200 times a second, constantly readjusting with new inputs from the senses (i.e., reality). Individual neurons with their own agendas and limitless internal storage capacity begin to interact in new ways. This resonance or harmony rises above individual neurons to create a new phenomenon—the mind, the parallel universe, the simulation—with its own rules that impose top-down, nondeterministic constraints on our possibilities for action. Again, "feeling".

Each human trait has both a "feeling" side and a cold algorithmic side. Above, I describe where "feeling" comes from: the mind is a parallel universe that stays synchronized with reality—through resonance—and perturbances in the simulation affect our ability to act. It may seem an unsatisfying answer, but as every schoolchild knows, we can't define a word in terms of itself. We can't describe *"feeling"* in terms of feeling.

In any case, I hope this understanding of "feeling" will release us—free us—so we can focus exclusively on the cold algorithms behind human traits. We must decouple "feeling" from the practical trait outcomes. If we want to know why happiness "feels" happy, or why sadness "feels" sad, we can simply reread this section. For every trait and emotion, "feeling" has the same explanation.

Consciousness

We don't consciously decide what happens in the brain. Billions of empowered independent neurons are busy doing their job by sending messages back and forth to other neurons and making decisions, large and small. Choices are made locally by neurons running their ancient programming—algorithms, loops, if–then–else conditionals, variable assignments, and the like—in the context of sensory inputs, in resonance with all the other neurons in the brain.

In other words, most of our decisions are made subconsciously, by individual neurons. Consciousness is mostly unaware of the vastness of the mind's parallel universe and the many corners of ubiquitous "chatter" in the brain.

Keeping with the theme of this book, I'll assume human consciousness is implemented by a single neuron, as follows:

```
class ConsciousnessNeuron:
    def ____init____(self):
        # Consciousness is merely our current location
        # or neural focal point in the mental simulation.
        self.consciousness = [] # e.g. ["neuron3","neuron54", …]
```

```
def sendrequest(self, requestor, reqtype, parameters):
    # allow any neuron to suggest itself
    # as an object of our consciousness
    if reqtype == "append":
        self.consciousness.append(requestor)
        # not so fast... need to prioritize somehow

def run(self):
    loop forever:
        loop for c in self.consciousness:
            # do something with the current
            # object of consciousness
            sendrequest(c, "raise priority", 100)
        wait(clocktick)
    # repeat loop
```

Consciousness is merely a pointer to a specific set of subconscious activities. It's a mental location described by a list of neurons currently receiving our focus—for example, "neuron3", "neuron54" .... As our consciousness shifts, the array values change.

For example, if we're hungry, our consciousness focuses on hunger to the exclusion of all else and raises its priority:

```
self.consciousness = ["HungerNeuron"]
```

As specific neurons receive priority, the entire mental simulation must readjust. That brief wobble in the mind's simulation is the conscious experience of "feeling".

[I've glossed over an obvious problem here. Surely—like little children—every neuron wants to be the center of conscious attention and have our highest-priority focus. Another algorithm is needed to consider and prioritize such requests. That is left as an exercise for the reader.]

That's all there is to consciousness. Consciousness is simply our current location in the mental simulation, a vector coordinate in the parallel universe of the mind. Consciousness is trivial.

Happiness Is a Sieve

Most of us can fake a smile by raising the corners of our mouth, but very few can voluntarily contract the muscles that surround the eyes. In a genuine (or Duchenne) smile, we contract the orbicularis oculi muscle, which forms wrinkles—crow's-feet—as our eyes close, and our cheeks move upward. We can't fake a genuine smile.

Happiness is often described as the emotional state we achieve when we're satisfied or content with our situation in life. Unfortunately, we're never happy for very long. Even lottery winners are only happy for six months, and then eventually they revert to their previous happiness level, whatever that was. Happiness is a sieve; its content slowly drips away.

In a previous section, I provided my own explanation of where qualia or "feeling" comes from. So there's no need to repeat it or dwell on the "feeling" of happiness here. That problem is solved. This leaves us free to focus on the inputs and outputs and algorithms of happiness.

Let's assume happiness and contentment arise when we complete our goals. Our HappinessNeuron continually checks whether we have any remaining goals in life or if we recently completed a goal. In either case, we're happy or at least content. Happiness causes the orbicularis oculi muscle—via a neuron of the same name—around the eye to contract. That's our way of letting others know we're happy. The code looks like this:

```
class HappinessNeuron:
    def ___init___(self):
        # begin life with no goals
        self.goals = []
        # and be happy!
        self.happiness _level = 100

    def run(self):
        loop forever:
            # happiness is a leaky sieve,
            # so subtract 1 from itself
            # each time through the loop
            self.happiness _level -= 1
            recently _completed _goal = False
```

```
loop for goal in self.goals:
    # check each goal for completion
    recent = sendrequest(goal, "recently complete")
    if recent == True:
        recently_completed_goal = True
        continue
# end goal loop
if recently_completed_goal == True or self.
goals == []:
    # we recently completed a goal,
    # or we completed all our goals,
    # so be happy!
    self.happiness_level = 100
    # genuine smile
    sendrequest("OrbicularisOculiNeuron", "contract")
    # what else?
wait(clocktick)
# repeat loop
```

That's it? Happiness is a contraction of the eye muscles? What's next? What's the practical effect of happiness?

As discussed earlier, happiness is an opening up of our energies and capabilities. When we're happy, we're more inclined to go for a walk, flirt with the neighbor, or put down the top of the convertible. So how does happiness open up our capabilities? How can it induce us to sing in the rain?

Here's how: neurons throughout the brain must be notified (signaled) to let them know it's okay to open up. There are two ways to accomplish this notification: push or pull. With push, the HappinessNeuron broadcasts a message to every neuron in the brain to let loose. (For network optimization purposes, this message might be accomplished by sending a neurotransmitter into the bloodstream that acts like a "smoke signal," visible to every neuron in the brain.) With pull, it's the responsibility of each neuron in the brain to ask the HappinessNeuron for permission— by sending it a request—before acting all happy.

My bias is push. To make the HappinessNeuron fully accountable for all happiness activity in the brain, it must be the initiator. This also makes sense from an evolutionary perspective. When happiness first evolved, it was highly localized in the brain. It would be much more difficult for evolution to implement pull, which would require a programming change to every existing neuron in the brain. That is, it would have to add code to request permission from the HappinessNeuron every time it wished to open up.

Therefore, the HappinessNeuron must maintain a list of every capability (neuron) in the brain affected by happiness, positively or negatively, and send it a message when it's time to be happy:

```
for n in self.happiness_dependent_neurons:
    sendrequest(n, "affect priority", +1)
```

Each neuron can decide what to do with its greater "affect priority." Perhaps it's a type of currency or bribe that can be paid to the ConsciousnessNeuron or PlannerNeuron (discussed later) to get bumped to the top of the priority list.

Disgust

Young children find feces fascinating as if it were clay to mold into playful shapes or seal cracks in their crib. Quickly, however, children develop a disgust for feces.

> Sometime in early childhood, a switch is thrown and children become like adults, disgusted by much of the world … Children come to find feces gross, and this insight isn't dependent on observing an adult's reaction … Disgust isn't learned but rather emerges naturally once babies have reached a certain point in development. (Bloom 2013)

The "yuck face" and "feeling" of nausea is universal. The smell of rotting meat is universally repugnant and triggers disgust. On the other hand, the object of disgust is sometimes learned. Some societies happily consume dog meat, for example, but the thought of eating Fido makes me want to gag.

So let's consider the two types of disgust:

```
class RottenMeatNeuron:
    def ___init___(self):
        # begin life with the instinct
        # to be repulsed by the smell of rotten meat
        self.scent _pattern = [[32, 77, 46]]

        def run(self):
            loop forever:
                s = sendrequest("NoseNeuron", "getvalue")
                if s in scent _pattern:
                    sendrequest("YuckFaceNeuron", "go")
                    sendrequest("WithdrawReflexNeuron", "go")
        wait(clocktick)
    # repeat loop
```

The smell of rotten meat is a simple sensory pattern, an array of numbers, picked up by special sensors in the nose. Humans can recognize 10,000 different odors via receptors connected to the olfactory nerve. All humans must perceive the smell of rotten meat as the same sensory pattern; otherwise, this ancient comparison code wouldn't work. The array (32, 77, 46) is hardwired into the DNA of every human, so it had better match up with the way we perceive the world.

(As with most other examples in this book, a fair dose of imagination and poetic license is applied. The neural coding examples are not meant to be taken literally, but instead are intended to demonstrate the possibilities. No one knows exactly what the neural code looks like.)

The second type of disgust involves a culturally learned target. For example, the thought of eating dog meat makes me disgusted and nauseous, not because I've experienced it, but because I've never seen anyone eating dog:

```
class FamiliarFoodsNeuron:
    def ___init___(self):
        # start life with an empty list of familiar foods
        self.familiar _foods = []

    def run(self):
        loop forever:
```

```
        food    =    sendrequest("EatingNeuron",
        "getcontent")
        if food not in self.familiar_foods:
            sendrequest("YuckFaceNeuron", "go")
            sendrequest("WithdrawReflexNeuron", "go")
    wait(clocktick)
# repeat loop
```

Our ancient DNA knows nothing about eating dog meat. It simply favors foods that we've seen someone else eating or that our parents fed us as children. This example demonstrates how we can have an evolved reaction—disgust—to a learned experience.

(I've omitted the code for the learning process behind the `self.familiar_food` list, but it might resemble how the `EnvyNeuron` establishes objects of envy in an earlier example.)

Fun fact: people with a high disgust response tend to vote Republican (McAuliffe 2019).

Pain

Pain is the unpleasant "feeling" associated with tissue damage. The "feeling" of pain derives from a disturbance in the brain's simulation of reality. However, since we've already discussed the nature of "feeling" in an earlier section, there's no need to revisit the topic. We can consider pain simply in terms of inputs and outputs.

Pain thus becomes a behavior to withdraw from potentially damaging situations while the body heals. With pain, for example, we simply can't move a broken arm. We lose our ability to choose to move it. Something in the brain stops us. We are constrained in our possibilities of motion.

The algorithm to implement pain could be distributed or centralized. In other words, pain could be implemented by a single `PainNeuron` in the brain or by multiple distributed neurons: a `FingerPainNeuron`, a `LegPainNeuron`, a `BackPainNeuron`, and so on.

Let's assume for the following example the existence of a single pain neuron in the brain:

```
class PainNeuron:
    def run(self):
        # get an inventory of all body parts
        body _parts = sendrequest("BodyPartsNeuron", "inventory")
        loop forever:
            for b in body _parts:
                i = sendrequest(b, "is inflammation")
                if i == True:
                    # what do we do now?
            wait(clocktick)
        # repeat loop
```

The PainNeuron queries each body part to determine the presence of inflammation associated with tissue damage. If such inflammation is present, then the PainNeuron has to somehow make that body part less functional and more constrained in its actions. Pain involves the shutting down of our ability to move. If the ArmNeuron plans for the arm to move, and if the arm is currently experiencing pain, the arm simply can't comply until the pain level is reduced.

That gives us a clue as to how pain can intervene with our plans. The arm's time is a scarce resource. Any requests to use the arm must pass through a PlannerNeuron (discussed later). So an easy way to limit the arm's mobility is to remove any of its plans for motion:

```
sendrequest("PlannerNeuron", "reset", b) # body part
```

This removes the arm from a queue of upcoming planned motions and thus leaves it motionless. This unexpected constraint creates a ripple effect throughout the brain's simulation as other neurons that had planned to use the arm—to play Frisbee, to stroke a lover's chin—have to scramble to make new plans. What a pain!

Hunger

During hunger, our stomach muscles contract in hunger pangs. We become weak. Again, we need not concern ourselves with the "feeling" of hunger.

Hunger is merely a shutting down of our capabilities (weakness) on one hand and a set of instinctual behaviors on the other hand as we initiate behavior to seek and ingest food. Here's the code:

```
class HungerNeuron:
    def run(self):
        loop forever:
            h = sendrequest("StomachNeuron", "hunger level")
            if h > 50:
                w = sendrequest("WalkOrRunNeuron", "is trained")
                if w == True:
                    sendrequest("PlannerNeuron", "reset")
                    sendrequest("SeekFoodNeuron", "go")
                else:
                    sendrequest("CryNeuron", "go")
            wait(clocktick)
        # repeat loop
```

The HungerNeuron queries the StomachNeuron to determine whether we're hungry. (It's more complicated than that, I know. A hormone called ghrelin is released if blood sugar levels get too low. But as mentioned previously, hormones and neurotransmitters are merely used for broadcast signals and network optimization. Identified neurons are the primary actors, and their messages are the primary conduits of information exchange in the brain.)

Keep in mind that the HungerNeuron algorithm is ancient, millions of years old, inherited from our ancestors. Evolution knew it could depend on a learned skill—walking and running—to seek food. As we saw earlier, that skill is associated with an identified neuron having a well-known name—WalkOrRunNeuron. A skill we learn in our lifetime is associated with a neuron whose name was assigned millions of years ago, so we know how to reference and exploit it.

According to the algorithm, if we're old enough to walk or run, then we go seek food. If not, then we cry, and hopefully an adult will bring us something to eat.

The seeking of food and the ingesting of it are different, decoupled instincts. Once food is located, the act of bringing it near to our eyes, nose, and mouth triggers a different instinct, to eat. In other words, seemingly disjointed instincts are rejoined in the context of the environment in which they evolved. The environment glues them together: behavior to observation to new behavior to new observation and so on.

```
class SeekFoodNeuron:
    def ___init___(self):
        # begin life clueless about what's edible
        self.edibles = []
        self.seeking_mode = False

    def sendrequest(self, requestor, reqtype, parameters):
        # reply to a request from another neuron
        # to seek food
        if reqtype == "go":
            self.seeking_mode = True

    def run(self):
        loop forever:
            if self.seeking_mode == False:
                # restart the loop
                continue
            else:
                f = sendrequest("PersonalSpaceNeuron", "getobject")
                if f in self.edibles:
                    sendrequest("PersonalSpaceNeuron", "grasp", f)
                else:
                    # keep walking
                    sendrequest("WalkOrRunNeuron", "go"):
            wait(clocktick)
            # repeat loop
```

The SeekFoodNeuron maintains a list of potential foods (edibles). Each edible is likely represented by a single trained FoodNeuron instance, utilizing a deep learning neural network that excels at pattern recognition. The current nearby objects (in our personal space) are compared to our list of known edibles. If an edible food is discovered, then we grasp it, and a different neuron (not shown) initiates the eating process and switches off the food-seeking mode. Otherwise, the WalkOrRunNeuron takes a few more steps and the loop repeats.

Obviously, this algorithm is underspecified. Comparison of a nearby object to a list of potential foods is a hard problem. And requesting the `WalkOrRunNeuron` to take a few more steps in search of food is also fraught. What if there's an open manhole cover or predator in our path?

To address this issue, identified neurons are granted a great deal of autonomy to accomplish their delegated tasks. For example, the `WalkOrRunNeuron` is responsible for identifying and avoiding obstacles, likely by delegating cognitive subtasks to other neurons. That's the power of object-oriented (agent-based) programming in a massively parallel system. Like a good manager, a neuron may delegate subtasks to other neurons, but it doesn't micromanage how those tasks are accomplished.

Depression

In 2018, there were over 128 suicides per day in the United States. Depression and other disorders are often the immediate cause. It's hard to think about depression in a detached and impersonal way. We often have personal experiences with depression or know family members or friends who are or were once afflicted.

Depression is associated with a "feeling" of hopelessness. It's not easy, but we have to leave "feeling" out of it for the purposes of this discussion. We need to be disciplined and focus only on the practical effect and behavior of depression.

Devoid of "feeling", what is depression? Does it have an evolutionary purpose? Perhaps it's a way to keep us still and quiet, such as after giving birth (hence postpartum depression); or its purpose is to give us time to reflect in the face of intractable challenges, like a death in the family; or it is meant to give us a sense of perspective from the valley and inspire us to climb to the mountaintop.

Depression and mania are opposites. It's a common control pattern in the brain to wire circuits in opposition, in order to maintain balance, yin and yang. For example, when one muscle in the arm, say the biceps muscle, contracts, an antagonist or opposite muscle, the triceps, extends. Having opposing muscle groups helps to maintain control. Without opposition, a muscle is unbalanced and goes haywire. So let's consider depression as a kind of control function to balance with mania.

How to implement depression as an algorithm? Let's assume depression is a reduction or closing down of possibilities in the brain. One way to do this is by overloading the brain's circuits with phony messages, like a denial of service (DoS) attack on the internet that takes down the servers of a website. The code would look something like this:

```
class DepressionNeuron:
    def ___init___(self):
        # wait, start life depressed???
        self.depression _level = 55

    def run(self):
        # get an inventory of all body parts
        body _parts = sendrequest("BodyPartsNeuron", "inventory")
        loop forever:
            if self.depression _level > 50:
                for b in body _parts:
                    sendrequest("PlannerNeuron", "go", b)
                wait(clocktick)
        # repeat loop
```

Perhaps the `DepressionNeuron` floods the brain—specifically, neurons that control the body—with spurious messages. The net effect is that all other neural messages have to compete for the same bodily resources and perhaps get deprioritized. One can imagine that the `StressNeuron` works the same way.

Devoid of its qualia or "feeling", depression is merely a shutting down of our ability to use bodily resources. Sounds so simple.

Love, Empathy, and Compassion

How does a mathematician choose a mate? It turns out there's a set of "optimal stopping" problems in mathematics that supplies a proven answer. (Originally, this was called the "secretary hiring problem," but I've modified it here.)

> Imagine you're interviewing a set of [potential mates], and your goal is to maximize the chance of [finding] the single best applicant in the pool ... You can decide to [propose] at any point and they are guaranteed to accept, terminating the search. But if you pass over [a potential mate], deciding not to [propose], they are gone forever. (Christian and Griffiths 2016)

Sort of takes the romance out of it! If the size of the applicant pool is 100, then how many do we interview before making a selection? It turns out that this problem has an answer: 37. In other words, interview 37 percent of the applicants to establish a baseline, and then immediately choose the next applicant who's better than all previous applicants.

We can even add more realistic assumptions to this love quest. If you have, say, a fifty-fifty chance of being rejected, then the same kind of mathematical analysis that yielded the 37 percent rule says you should start making offers after you are just a quarter of the way through your search.

Okay, okay, this all sounds very cold and clinical. Where's the love? Where's the empathy and compassion? (Sorry, re-read the previous section on "feeling" if needed.)

You now have the tools. Implementation of the `LoveNeuron`, `EmpathyNeuron`, and `CompassionNeuron` is left as an exercise for the reader.

PART 5—WHAT MAKES US HUMAN?

Abstract Thought

Children under twelve years old are literal and concrete thinkers. They see the world in terms of the here and now, as a series of unrelated events. They possess an amazing ability to memorize details, but they can't summarize or extract key themes and have a hard time with reading comprehension and intuiting what is important. Their mental model of the world is underdeveloped.

Psychologists from Erik Erikson to Jean Piaget have written about the stages of human psychosocial development from early childhood to adulthood; these stages appear to be universal across the human species. Each stage builds on the previous one. Perhaps abstract thinking isn't possible until concrete thinking is firmly established as a foundation.

Sometime around adolescence, children transition from being concrete thinkers to abstract thinkers. It's a dramatic metamorphosis of brain wiring, akin to how caterpillars (or teenagers) replace most of their brain when they transform into butterflies (or adults), yet somehow retain some early memories (Blackiston, Silva Casey and Weiss 2008). This is more proof that memories exist independently from neural connections.

Not coincidentally, the onset of schizophrenia often occurs around adolescence, when the brain is rewiring itself for more abstract thought. In schizophrenia, people become disconnected from reality, become detached from specific social interactions, and believe thoughts are being inserted into their minds.

Not to be glib, but that's exactly what abstract thinking is. New thoughts—models, themes, ideas, unseen actors—are introduced in the brain and float above the concrete reality of everyday events. The challenge is to make the transition successfully and relate these new thoughts to an explanatory framework for reality without getting lost and disconnected from this framework. Failure to succeed at this results in mental illness.

Abstract thought requires mental models. We adults constantly attempt to make sense of our observations by fitting them into a mental model, determining cause and effect, and finding patterns and analogies.

One example of a model is used in storytelling. When we go to the movies, we have an expectation of a specific story model or structure, and if we don't find it, we lose interest. Hollywood caters to this innate need. If we observe closely, we'll see that every movie adheres to the same three-act structure containing the same fifteen beats (Snyder 2005):

- act 1—opening image, theme stated, setup, catalyst, debate
- act 2—leave the old world behind, fun and games, B story, midpoint, bad guys close in, all hope is lost, dark night of the soul
- act 3—all enemies vanquished, finale

In a 110-page screenplay, act 2 always begins on page 25. The "all hope is lost" moment always shows up on page 75 (i.e., approximately 75 minutes into the movie); otherwise, the audience grows bored. In the movie *Star Wars*, for example, the mentor character Obi-Wan dies on page 75 in the script, right on cue.

In storytelling, we also expect the presence of certain archetypal characters. *Star Wars* delivers the hero (Luke), the mentor/sage (Obi-Wan or Yoda), the rebel (Han Solo), the jester (C-3PO), and so forth (Campbell 2014).

We enjoy movies that adhere to this standard model. Movies that don't follow the pattern—hardwired in our brain—usually bomb at the box office.

Abstract thinking is simply a set of models (such as the storytelling model). Sometimes models develop earlier, and sometimes they develop later, in the brain. A mental model doesn't require learning, although it may require fine-tuning and instantiation. And each mental model—by my theory—is represented by a single identified neuron in the brain that loads and runs its complex programming instructions and algorithms from our shared DNA library.

Implementation of the StoryNeuron that represents our preferred storytelling model in the brain is left as an exercise for the reader.

Planning and Scheduling

We only have two hands, ten fingers, two legs, two eyes, and a finite amount of time on this planet. Neurons in the brain compete for the use of these scarce bodily resources to perform their tasks, like "retrieve food" or "kill invader" or "seek a mate."

We can't do everything at once. A request—to move a finger or a leg or an eye—must be prioritized. When multiple neurons simultaneously require the use of the eyes—for example, "stare down a foe" and simultaneously "flirtatiously roll eyes at a potential mate"—the requests must be queued accordingly.

Let's assume the existence of a single PlannerNeuron in the brain that allocates available time buckets for each resource on a master schedule. (Keep in mind that examples in this book are offered more as concepts than as fully realized and scientifically proven theories.)

```
class PlannerNeuron:
    def ___init___(self):
        # start life with an empty schedule - nice!
        self.schedule = []
```

```
def sendrequest(self, requestor, reqtype, parameters):
    # receive a request from another neuron
    # to schedule a task, e.g., "move finger"
    if reqtype == "go":
        self.schedule.append(parameters)
    elsif reqtype == "reset":
        # remove things from the schedule
        if parameters != False:
            self.schedule.remove(parameters)
        else:
            self.schedule = [] # remove everything

def run(self):
    loop forever:
        for task in self.schedule:
            (object, priority, start, due, params) = task
            # continually review or replan each task
            # to maintain an optimal schedule
            ... code not shown
        # Check the current time on our internal clock
        now = sendrequest("ClockNeuron", "getvalue")
        for task in self.schedule:
            # a task is basically a message to
            # another neuron at a later time
            (object, priority, start, due, params) = task
            if start < now:
                # when the task's start time is reached
                # send a message to the object as planned
                sendrequest(object, "go", params)
        wait(clocktick)
    # repeat loop
```

Any neuron can propose a new task to the `PlannerNeuron` for scheduling. A scheduled task is merely a message to be sent to another neuron at a future time. An internal `ClockNeuron` is used to globally synchronize planned and actual task start times.

Planning and scheduling solutions are well-known in the field of operations research (OR). Scheduling strategies include "process earliest due date tasks first" and "process shortest processing time tasks first" (Pinedo 2016). Airlines, for example, use scheduling algorithms to optimally fill available seats on flights and adjust ticket prices to control demand. A canceled flight requires an immediate replanning of the master schedule, and passengers are reassigned to seats on other flights. The gate is freed up for use by other aircraft.

Likewise, the brain's `PlannerNeuron` continually reviews the proposed task start times and priorities and establishes a new plan to ensure resources are not overallocated. Two requests that are in conflict—for example, turn both eyeballs left and right simultaneously—require a replan.

Language

Linguist Noam Chomsky famously declared that the acquisition of human language is an innate and evolved capability (Chomsky 1957). We simply can't acquire language from experience alone because those inputs are relatively impoverished. When we hear someone speak, we often don't hear every word clearly, yet children pick up language quickly and naturally (Pinker 1994). Therefore, language acquisition must have a built-in algorithmic assist.

To disambiguate words, the algorithm likely maintains a list of word frequencies and words commonly paired together. That would allow us to fill in missing words. The word *house* is more common than *grouse*, and the words *upper* and *hand* are more commonly paired together to form a phrase than *copper* and *hand*.

We're prewired to learn and generate grammar as well. We can generate an infinite number of syntactically valid sentences—such as "I went," "I went to the place," and "I went to the place I went yesterday"—using universal grammar rules.

Grammar can be formally defined. A sentence (S) may consist of a noun phrase (NP) and a verb phrase (VP). A verb phrase may consist of a verb (V) and a noun phrase (NP) with a determiner (Det) like "the", or it may be recursively defined (VP PP), allowing for an endless variety of grammatical sentence structures, as follows:

S → NP VP

PP → P NP

NP → Det N | Det N PP

VP → V NP | VP PP

Sentences consist of tokens (i.e., words) that are tagged with their corresponding parts of speech. For example, the word *kite* is usually a noun, but it can also be used as a verb, as in "kite a check." I'm not a computational linguist, so I won't attempt to write a natural language processing (NLP) algorithm. The good news is there are many excellent books available on NLP using Python (Bird, Klein and Loper 2009).

Words are also associated with meanings or semantic concepts. The easiest way to convey meaning is through example. A child may ask, "Mommy, what is pushing?" and in response the mother lightly pushes her child and says, "It's like that." When our caregiver points at an object and speaks a word, we effortlessly identify the object he or she references and associate the sound with it. Humans have a mental model for such references.

Words themselves (as signifiers) must be learned, but the word learning process is an evolved ability in humans. Other species don't have it. If we point out an object to a dog, it simply licks our finger. And we humans don't even require vocalized speech. Words can be associated with any number of sense perceptions. Sign language employs visual representations instead of sounds to denote words.

How do we associate meaning with words and grammar? The philosopher Jerry Fodor believed all lexical concepts are primitive and thus innate (Fodor 1975). No primitive concept can be learned unless the brain is prewired to learn it. Words have no meaning unless they can be associated with innate concepts.

What does this mean? Nobody can teach us a concept like the color red unless we're already hardwired to learn it. The same holds true for all primitive concepts. This is a stunning and controversial observation by Fodor. Every learnable concept—numbers, objects, causality, agency—comes with a prewired mental model or algorithm in the brain. If that algorithm—wrapped inside an identified neuron—doesn't exist, then we can't learn the concept. Complex concepts are only learnable if they can be expressed in terms of innate primitive concepts.

As I mentioned earlier, the philosopher Plato asked in his dialogue *Meno* how we can begin to learn anything if we have no notion about what is to be learned. The answer is that we can't. We receive algorithms—the language of thought (LOT), as Fodor put it—from our ancestors for each learnable concept.

Rationality

Our choices and decisions—all of them—originate from our impulses, fears, passions, needs, compulsions, and desires. Each of these traits is implemented by a single, local, identified neuron in the brain according to my theory. Identified neurons selfishly and doggedly pursue their own agenda. They are responsible and accountable for achieving their goals and objectives, in competition with every other neuron in the brain for scarce bodily resources.

This highly distributed decision-making activity occurs subconsciously. We simply can't be consciously aware of the activity of every neuron of the brain. Consciousness, as discussed earlier, is simply our current location in the mental simulation or parallel universe. Unity of mind is achieved by the resonance—or stable state—of the mind's simulation with reality.

To present a facade of rationality for the thousands of subconscious decisions and choices made by independent neural actors (agents), the brain has evolved a separate capability to spin elaborate yarns and rationalizations:

> A specialized system [in the brain] called the "interpreter"
> generates explanations about our perceptions, memories,
> and actions ... Its drive to generate hypotheses is the
> trigger for human beliefs, which, in turn, constrain our
> brain ... This is a post hoc rationalization process ... How
> much of the time are we confabulating, giving a fictitious

account of a past event, believing it to be true? (Gazzaniga 2011, 102)

The interpreter—or confabulator, or rationalizer—serves up after-the-fact justifications for our subconscious actions and beliefs. After we become consciously aware of our actions, the interpreter weaves a plausible-sounding story for us to explain our actions to others:

> The interpreter provides the storyline and narrative, and we all believe we are agents acting of our own free will, making important choices. The illusion is so powerful that there is no amount of analysis that will change our sensation that we are all acting willfully and with purpose. (Gazzaniga 2011, 105)

Human language is thus not used to convey objective facts about the world. We're notoriously unreliable when it comes to explaining the causes for and motivations behind our actions or uncovering true causes for everyday events. Instead, the purpose of language is to bind us together as a society, enforce cultural norms, and help us survive.

How is the interpreter implemented in the brain? Does each identified neuron have the ability to justify its own actions? Or is there a central rationalizer—a `RationalizationNeuron`—that generates plausible-sounding, socially acceptable explanations for why we do what we do? In other words, is rationalization distributed or centralized?

If distributed, for example, the `AweNeuron` would have to generate plausible justifications for its own actions. Every mental model and every innate concept would have to explain itself for social purposes, even if the explanation may bear no relationship to the underlying intent of the model itself. It's like the politician who tells his audience, "You're the finest people I've ever met, and I am your humble servant," but who really means "I'll say anything to get your vote and further my own ambition."

If rationalization is centralized, on the other hand, a single `InterpreterNeuron` (or `ModelInterpreterNeuron`) would generate all the blarney, confabulations, and justifications for every identified neuron in the brain. I think it's more plausible, from an evolutionary point of view, that a single neuron is responsible for a single task. But that's a big task!

Reasoning

We humans like to think of ourselves as logical thinkers. For thousands of years, philosophers from Aristotle to Gottlob Frege have dabbled with syllogistic reasoning and formalized predicate logic, as follows:

1. For all x, if x is a man, then x is mortal. $\forall x:[\text{Man}(x) \rightarrow \text{Mortal}(x)]$
2. Socrates is a man. Man(Socrates)
3. It follows that Socrates is mortal. Mortal(Socrates)

Such formal logic offered the promise of inferences that neatly chained together. All men are mortal. All mortals are hungry. All hungry people seek food. And so on. But such logical chaining proved to be quite fragile in the real world. Then, in the 20th century, along came Gödel's "incompleteness theorem" and Heisenberg's "uncertainty principle," and attempts at formal reasoning collapsed.

Humans are not terribly logical. No news there. The "four-card problem" illustrates the imperfect way we engage in purely deductive reasoning:

> Four cards are placed on a table. Each card has a number on one side and a colored patch on the other side. The four visible faces show 3, 8, red, and brown. You are told a rule: "If a card has an even number on one face, then the opposite face is red." Which card or cards must you turn over to test whether the rule has been broken? (Wikipedia, Wason Selection Task)

The correct answer is to turn over the 8 card *and* the brown card. Only 10 percent of people get this right. We don't intuitively know that "if A, then B" is equivalent to "if not B, then not A," so we forget to turn over the brown card. Also, we erroneously believe that "if A, then B" implies "if not A, then not B" and mistakenly turn over the 3 card instead.

However, in social settings, we find the same rule more intuitive. The rule is "If you are drinking alcohol, then you must be over eighteen," and the cards have an age on one side and beverage on the other—for example, sixteen, drinking beer, twenty-five, drinking Coke. Most people have no difficulty in selecting the correct cards (sixteen and drinking beer). It turns out we have an innate mental model for a logically equivalent question when applied to "policing a social rule" (Barkow, Cosmides and Tooby 1992).

Our mental models are built for survival and social interaction. We don't engage in purely formal logic.

The mind has a different way of working: incrementally. We take an action or make a modest inference or assertion and then sit back and observe the outcome. Based on the new reality, we adjust and take a new action or make a new assertion based on the evidence. In other words, we constantly bounce our ideas and actions off reality and then modify our next action based on feedback from the environment.

Reasoning, then, becomes a series of heuristics, or guesses, or stabs in the dark. Try something, observe the results, and then try something new based on those results. We constantly resynchronize our mental simulation with environmental inputs to maintain a tight connection with reality.

Each neuron runs a short and disconnected program containing loops, variable assignments (memory), and if–then–else conditionals. After each iteration of a loop, the program waits for a moment to sniff the environment for new sensory inputs, as well as messages from other neurons. The brain must constantly resynchronize its simulation with reality. Its internal state is defined by resonance, not logic.

Reason is not a triumph over the emotions. It's just a model that aids our survival.

Gossip

Gossip is about communicating who is doing what to whom. It has a powerful social and evolutionary purpose. Beyond the exchange of salacious details, gossip provides a powerful means of control over our leaders; it enforces social norms, and it shames aberrant behavior. It's true that (almost) no one wants to be the target of vicious rumors, so fear of gossip keeps us in line.

Gossip also requires that our social expectations and predictions not be met. When we're surprised by what someone else did—abusing power, having a secret affair—we want to tell someone else:

```
class GossipNeuron:
    def ___init___(self):
        # start life with nothing to gossip about
        self.gossip = []

    def sendrequest(self, requestor, reqtype, parameters):
        # Allow another neuron to send us gossip
        # using a standard format
        if reqtype == "add":
            # Now we have something to gossip about!
            (who, what, to_whom, when, source) = parameters
            self.gossip.append(parameters)
```

Gossip takes the format (who, what, to_whom, when, source). As it arrives, it's appended to our existing knowledge bank of gossip. This content is then fed into our language capability as fodder the next time we're chatting with a gossip partner.

This code can obviously get very complex, very quickly. We need to maintain a list of gossip partners we trust with enough discretion not to pass along rumors to the wrong person (of course that never happens!). We also need to remember whom we told what so we don't repeat ourselves. Gossip can be refuted or retracted, so we need a way to remove it from the list (that never happens either!).

Any takers to write the rest of the code?

Creativity

Creativity and invention are said to be defining human characteristics. We humans harnessed fire, domesticated animals, and invented many things, including agriculture, the wheel, writing, and mathematics. We devised labor-saving tools, nuclear power, computers, and the internet, and we've walked on the moon.

In agriculture, scientific discoveries such as selective breeding and crop genetics have improved crop yield and efficiency to such a degree that only 2 percent of the US population are now farmers. Similar labor displacements await if self-driving cars, taxis, and trucks become reality.

However, creativity isn't unique to humans. Even birds have invented tools. A carpenter finch, for example, can make a tool from a twig or cactus spine and insert it into tree bark to extract a grub to eat.

I believe invention is a three-step process:

1. Idea generation
2. Idea recognition and testing
3. Idea communication

To generate new ideas, we dream. We freely associate our memories and mental models, without an internal censor and unconstrained by our current way of thinking, to uncover new configurations and combinations.

For example, how did Albert Einstein come up with his theory of special relativity? He used a thought experiment. He imagined a moving train being struck by lightning in the front and rear. From the perspective of observers outside the train, the two lightning strikes were simultaneous, but train passengers saw a time lag between the two strikes. In other words, what we perceive is relative to where we're standing (our reference frame). A high school student can grasp this insight with some training, but it was a staggeringly creative insight at the time. Einstein had to combine rather mundane ideas—lightning and trains, in the context of a recent scientific discovery that the speed of light is constant—in novel ways.

After an idea is generated, we recognize and test its utility and application in the real world, or we discard it. This process can be brutal and probabilistic. Ten entrepreneurs may generate ten different ideas, all funded and incubated by angel investors and venture capitalists. But the ultimate utility of each idea is tested in the court of public opinion, measured by popularity and sales of new products or through a stock offering on the public market. Unfortunately, nine out of ten ideas fail to catch the public's imagination, and most companies go out of business. The successful entrepreneur is lucky to have correctly guessed the public's mood.

Many entrepreneurs attempt to protect their ideas and intellectual property (IP) through patents, copyrights, and trademarks. But ideas are easy to copy and hard to defend against counterfeiting. The inventor of fire, for example, likely had a curious crowd gathered around him: "Oh, I see, you strike flint against iron and create sparks and fire? That's so simple I could have thought of it myself!"—and they run away and tell their neighbors and copy the experiment.

Some ideas take longer to catch on. For example, Chinese Taoists discovered gunpowder around 300 AD, yet it took them 700 years to realize it could be used for weapons. But eventually most compelling ideas spread like wildfire.

Let's explore the mind of the finch that invented a tool to extract grubs from a tree. Perhaps we humans are creative in the same way:

```
class CreativityNeuron:
    def run(self):
        loop forever:
            # get a list of all neurons in the brain
            # (I know, this code is not optimized!)
            all_neurons = sendrequest("GenesisNeuron",
            "inventory")
            for n in all_neurons:
                # ping each neuron,
                # for brief conscious awareness
                sendrequest(n, "ping")
            wait(clocktick)
        # repeat loop
```

That's it? Yes and no. This code implements only the generative aspect of creativity. The algorithm pings each identified neuron—each model—in the brain, one at a time, and raises it to brief conscious awareness in the hopes that the right two or three ideas will land simultaneously in working memory.

Then the testing aspect of creativity takes over, and hopefully a vital connection is made. As we're briefly made aware of neural models in the brain, we mull them over quickly: *I hadn't thought of that. Where did that idea come from?* In Einstein's case: *Trains, lightning ... aha!* Then, just as quickly, we forget. The passing thought flits away unless it resonates with the current problem to be solved.

Another example: Assume we're grappling with the problem of how to make our pushcart more efficient. The `CircleNeuron` in the brain is randomly pinged. Our consciousness is presented with two simultaneous ideas: circles and pushcarts. In our mental simulation, the two ideas begin to resonate and bounce off each other. How can circles make our pushcart go faster? Pretty soon, we have a eureka moment—we've invented the wheel!

So now let me blow your mind: Some insights may happen more slowly, over thousands of generations. The trick is to retain partial insights and pass them along to the next generation so they can continue to work the problem. Partial solutions can potentially be transferred via germ-line DNA—as we saw in the earlier section on brain transfer—and passed down to our children to solve. Now there's a creative idea!

Advocacy

We've all seen someone who is completely convinced of his or her own cause. Such a person has complete faith—that is, a high expectation of success, also known as self-efficacy—in his or her ideas. Such a person's total conviction lends him or her a dominant posture. When we see this, we—like submissive monkeys—step aside, demur, and let this individual have his or her way (Bandura 1997).

People with high self-efficacy can become powerful proponents to proselytize, popularize, and communicate new ideas. Was the apostle Paul an effective advocate when he singlehandedly converted millions of people to Christianity? Definitely. He had complete confidence in his faith, and (I imagine) the look of absolute conviction on his face that helped him convince others. Again, we're hardwired to follow someone with high self-belief.

Five thousand years ago in the Middle East, there was a burst of creativity in the human mind. Writing—cuneiform script—was invented in Mesopotamia, replacing clay tablets used for counting and recording goods. Around that time, the wheel was also invented. Soon thereafter, monotheism—the belief in a single God—became the foundation of future Judeo-Christian and Muslim religions. The first laws were also established around that time. The Code of Hammurabi in ancient Mesopotamia contained 282 laws, mostly variations of "an eye for an eye, a tooth for a tooth," harsher if you were a slave or a woman, more lenient if you were free or a man.

Why the sudden burst of creativity—laws, numbers, writing, wheels—in such a short period of time? I believe humans began to value abstractions—belief in numbers and geometry, belief in a single god—more highly than they valued themselves. We became extreme advocates, willing to die for our ideas. Such advocacy is, perhaps, an extension of bravery in battle, when a heady cause, solidarity, and allegiance to authority outweigh an individual's sense of self-preservation.

The code might look something like this:

```
class AdvocacyNeuron:
    def ____init____(self):
        # let's say we're all born fanatics
        self.efficacy_level = 100

    def run(self):
        loop forever:
            if self.efficacy_level > 99:
                # turn off self-preservation
                sendrequest("SelfPreservationNeuron",
                "setvalue", 0)
                # what's next?
            wait(clocktick)
        # repeat loop
```

For an extreme advocate, abstract ideas—numbers, pure sounds, pure shapes, single deities—are more exciting than mundane daily experience. The advocate is willing to proselytize these ideas even at grave risk to his or her own life.

For example, the philosopher Socrates willingly accepted his death sentence—by drinking poison hemlock—for questioning the powerful and the gods. The Italian philosopher Giordano Bruno was burned at the stake for suggesting that the earth revolves around the sun, rather than vice versa. English politician Algernon Sidney was beheaded for questioning the absolute godlike power of the king. Women from the philosopher Hypatia to Rosa Parks chose to fight for human rights at great personal risk and sacrifice. Each had an opportunity to recant yet chose to accept their fate rather than disavow their beliefs.

In reality, only a small percentage of the population—think Steve Jobs— are designated by evolution to be extreme advocates, or at least good marketers of ideas. Any more and we'd have chaos. But without a few zealots around, we'd have no entrepreneurs and no innovators. Modern society would slowly regress, deteriorate, decline, and stagnate. Having the right balance of fanatics and followers makes progress possible, even as it sets the stage for role differentiation and inequality, as we'll see later.

Common Sense

We know many things to be obvious: Objects fall when we release them. Reality exists outside our mental simulation. Real objects persist through time. We can't be in two different places at once. The past has existence. Water is wet.

However, we may not know that common sense and innate mental models are the same thing. As discussed earlier, each learnable concept must be associated with a mental model—an identified neuron running an innate algorithm. Otherwise we can't learn it. Common sense is no different. It's common because we all share the same DNA from where the algorithms are loaded.

For the past thirty years, computer scientist Douglas Lenat has been creating common sense algorithms. His team developed CYC, an encyclopedic knowledge base containing thousands of hand-engineered default rules of common sense and domain-specific expert judgment (Knight 2016). Lenat believes all knowledge is logically consistent. He advocates an "inference engine capable of producing hundreds-deep chains of deduction and induction."

I think that's the wrong approach. Knowledge about the world is complex, messy, conflicting, and inconsistent. As I wrote earlier, formal logic offered the promise of inferences that neatly chained together, but such logical chaining proves to be quite fragile in the real world.

An alternate approach taken by researcher Oren Etzioni is "paying crowdsourced humans on Amazon Mechanical Turk to help craft common-sense statements" (Thompson 2018). But I advocate an agent-based simulation approach.

Regardless of how it's implemented, our common sense is often wrong and misguided because we apply ancient wisdom to modern situations. For example, we greatly overestimate risk, especially in situations involving dread (or powerlessness) or long-term pain, even though these occurrences are extremely rare:

> The decision to drive instead of fly is a common example ... Behind the wheel [of a car], we're in charge; in the passenger seat of a crowded airline, we might as well be cargo. So white-knuckle flyers routinely choose the car, heedless of the fact that at most a few hundred people die in U.S. commercial airline crashes in a year, compared with 44,000 killed in motor-vehicle wrecks. (Kluger 2006)

Common sense evolved when we lived in small bands of hunter-gatherers. There were no airplanes back then. Sometimes our ancient models get in the way of modern life.

Cause and Effect

The philosopher David Hume said there's no necessary connection between any two events and that correlation doesn't imply causation.

I disagree. We're born with a preexisting mental model for cause and effect. For example, the experimental psychologist Albert Michotte showed children two blocks, one of which was moving toward a second, stationary block (Michotte 1946/1963). The experiment had several variations. A first group of children saw the moving block make physical contact with the second block, after which the second block immediately launched in the same direction. A second group of children saw the same thing, except an artificial delay was introduced between the contact and the launch. A third group of children saw the first block stop before making contact, yet the second block still launched. The experiment was later repeated with nonsolid objects such as beams of light (Carey 2009).

It was discovered that young children easily learn that direct physical contact between a moving and stationary object *causes* the second object to move. It's much harder for them to learn causality when a gap in time or space is present. And when some concepts are easier to learn than others, we can assume that humans have a preexisting mental model; otherwise, all experiences would be equally learnable.

Let's assume a single `CauseAndEffectByContactNeuron` implements physical contact perception in the brain:

```
class CauseAndEffectByContactNeuron:
    def ___init___(self):
        # start life with an empty list of causes and effects
        self.causes _and _effects = []

    def run(self):
        loop forever:
            m = sendrequest("MovingObjectNeuron", "detect")
            s = sendrequest("StationaryObjectNeuron", "detect")
            c = sendrequest("ContactNeuron", "detect", (m,s))
            l = sendrequest("MovingObjectNeuron", "detect", s)
            if m and s and c and l:
```

```
      self.causes _and _effects.append([m,s])
   wait(clocktick)
# repeat loop
```

When we observe a moving object making contact with a stationary object, resulting in the launch of the latter object, we add it to our memory of causes and effects. Without this innate concept—that is, model or algorithm—we wouldn't be able to form this memory.

Not all causes and effects require a mental model, however. A baby cries not in anticipation of food but because he's hungry. The baby doesn't need to know that crying causes the caregiver to feed him. Two instincts may, instead, rely on the environmental context to link them together.

Risk-Taking

Humans reached Australia by boat around 50,000 years ago. At the time, boats were extremely primitive—made of bamboo—and were not designed for ocean travel. A small group of fanatics (or, more accurately, a small group of fanatics and their trusting loved ones) packed up their belongings and headed off into the unknown ocean, willing to risk everything.

Human expansion and migration—perhaps even the long-term survival of the species—relied on having a few extreme risk-takers in the population. But the cost was likely enormous. Most of the intrepid souls likely died before a lucky few succeeded. Extreme risk-taking behavior is beneficial to society even as it's detrimental to the longevity of individuals.

In the same way as our ancestors, entrepreneurs are big risk-takers. The successful ones—Steve Jobs, Bill Gates, Mark Zuckerberg, Jeff Bezos—become household names. But nine out of ten fail and are often forgotten or lose everything. (The resilient ones get back on their feet and try again.)

Some psychiatrists suggest that neurotransmitters or genetic variations "cause" such entrepreneurial or risk-taking behavior:

> Associated with high levels of dopamine [is] excessive involvement in high-risk, pleasure-seeking activities ...

People who have a long form of the DRD4 gene, such as
the 7R allele [gene variant], are more likely to take risks.
(Lieberman and Long 2018)

I think this is exactly backward. Dopamine is just a molecule like water
or oxygen. It's not an algorithm or model. By itself, it can't plan or have
desires. It's just a signal, a puff of smoke.

I concede that genetic variation appears to explain about 20 percent of
the individual variation in risk-taking behavior (Dreberab and Apicellac
2009). Since risk-taking and novelty-seeking behaviors are ancient, perhaps
evolution originally implemented them using gene variants. However,
we humans now have so many innate models and traits it's likely that
evolution switched to a more scalable approach. I propose that human
behavioral traits are no longer associated with dedicated neurotransmitters
or gene variants. Rather, they are implemented in the brain via identified
neurons. Neurotransmitters simply optimize the messaging network
between neurons.

Let's assume, then, that risk-taking is implemented by a single
RiskTakingNeuron in the brain. The code would look something like
this:

```
class RiskTakingNeuron:
    def ___init___(self):
        # at or around birth, set our risk tolerance randomly
        # 0=risk averse, 100=extreme risk-taker
        # more on this later
        self.risk_tolerance = roll_the_dice(1,100)

    def sendrequest(self, requestor, reqtype, parameters):
        # Process an incoming request from another neuron
        # to query our risk tolerance
        # before planning an activity
        if reqtype == "getvalue":
            return self.risk_tolerance
```

This code is an example of a pull trait instead of a push trait. Other
neurons wishing to engage in risky behavior must first query the

`RiskTakingNeuron` before initiating action. If our risk tolerance is high, we will engage in risky behavior. If not, then not. However, I believe most traits are implemented as push, not pull. The code rewrite is left as an exercise for the reader.

Note that risk tolerance level is assigned algorithmically—by a roll of the dice—when the `RiskTakingNeuron` is first generated in the brain. In other words, variability in risk-taking behavior is not correlated with DNA variability but instead is assigned algorithmically. More on that later.

Talent

The most talented people are fanatically obsessed with practicing their craft. They enjoy it and find it fun, like a game.

Baseball great Ted Williams wasn't born swinging a bat (Schenk 2011). Through practice, practice, and more practice, he rewired his brain to perform expertly in the moment—like a doctor who studies for many years in order to make a complex diagnosis in the blink of an eye.

Why did Ted Williams succeed in baseball when other kids in his neighborhood didn't? Because he had greater persistence. He was obsessed and motivated. He had greater natural resilience, drive, motivation, and determination to stick with his practice routine—time on task. He used his charm to enlist other kids to help him practice, and he boldly approached other baseball greats for advice.

But not everyone is interested in—motivated by, passionate about—the same things. Most of us are not interested in swinging a baseball bat or in charming others to get our way. We're driven by other things. This leads us to spend more time on certain tasks than others. Spending more time on (different) tasks leads to (different) habits and skills and, eventually, (different) expertise and talent.

PART 6—TRAIT DIVERSITY

Moral Sentiments

The economist Adam Smith wrote that humans, by nature, are social animals. We feel happy when others are happy, and we feel sad when others are sad. We feel compassion and sorrow for the misery of others (Smith 1759).

Psychologist Jonathan Haidt suggests we're born with a moral sense—experiences like awe, gratitude, sympathy, compassion, empathy, guilt, shame, and embarrassment (Haidt 2012). These senses keep us bound together as a society. We feel guilty when we let each other down. We feel a sense of awe for authority figures and God. We feel shame when we step outside social norms. At least most of us do.

Even babies demonstrate moral traits without having to be taught (Bloom 2013). For example:

- a capacity to distinguish between kind and cruel actions
- empathy and compassion—suffering at the pain of those around us and the wish to make this pain go away
- a rudimentary sense of fairness—a tendency to favor equal divisions of resources
- a rudimentary sense of justice—a desire to see good actions rewarded and bad actions punished

Babies have a nascent sense of justice. In an experiment, a puppet was established as either a good guy or a bad guy. Then the puppet rolled a ball to a new puppet, which either retrieved the ball (i.e., acted nice) or ran away with it (i.e., acted mean).

> Eight-month-olds … preferred the puppet who was mean
> to the bad guy over the one who was nice to it. So at some
> point after five months, babies begin to prefer punishers—
> when the punishment is just. (Bloom 2013)

As usual, let's assume there's a single `JusticeNeuron` in the brain. Here's the (partial) code:

```
class JusticeNeuron:
    def ___init___(self):
        # begin life with an empty list
        # of observed bad actions
        self.bad _actions = []

    run(self):
        loop forever:
            # identify the bad actions nearby
            bad _action = sendrequest("BadActionNeuron",
            "isnearby")
            if bad _action == False:
                continue # restart the loop
            fair _punishment = False
            # decompose the action into who did what to whom
            (action2, by _person2, target _person2) = bad _action
            for b in self.bad _actions:
                # decompose previous bad actions
                (action1, by _person1, target _person1) = b
                if target _person2 == by _person1:
                    # the target of a mean action was
                    # a previously known bad actor, so
                    # justice is served!
                    fair _punishment = True
            if fair _punishment == False:
                # if not justifiable punishment, remember it
                self.bad _actions.append(bad _action)
            wait(clocktick)
        # repeat loop
```

In this simplistic model, we keep track of bad actions to be punished later. These actions are maintained in lists or arrays and stored inside the `JusticeNeuron` (i.e., written to local DNA memory storage). If a mean action is taken against someone who was previously mean to others, then it is considered fair punishment or due retribution.

Much of the detailed work in the neuron's program (above) is delegated to the `BadActionNeuron`, which in turn makes requests to perhaps dozens of other neurons in a great cascade of neural chain mail to support this justice model.

Why Do We Differ?

According to President Donald Trump (on *The Apprentice*), "People are born a certain way, and for the most part that's what you get". The former reality TV showman and casino magnate says he's a big believer in genetics as the source of his "very good brain" and that he's proud of his German genes (Fang and Rieger 2016).

Is Trump right? Do genetic variations account for human trait differences? Are group differences—for example, introverts and extroverts—the result of genetic differences?

No, I don't think so, although—*mea culpa!*—I used to believe this myself in the folly of my youth. Now, except for certain physical traits and genetic diseases, I no longer believe genetic variations are responsible for trait differences.

Why not? First of all, "genes" account for a relatively small amount—9 percent—of our DNA. We humans all have the same 20,000 genes, used to express proteins that construct the body. Only 2 percent of our DNA actually encodes those genes, and another 7 percent of our DNA helps to regulate that gene expression. So genetic variability is probably not the cause of trait variability.

Second, we humans are 99.9 percent alike in our DNA. That's not enough difference to account for human trait diversity in my view. We don't swap different DNA for different traits when we conceive children. We all have the same DNA. While it's possible that physical traits like height, hair color, and even athletic ability are partially heritable (D. Epstein 2014), I don't believe differences in mental traits are heritable. We're not like dogs, bred for our traits. We're more like female honeybees that can become either a worker or queen, depending on the context. (You may have heard of epigenetic tags, but I don't think they're responsible for trait diversity either because they're more associated with gene expression.)

However, humans do have highly variable traits across the population. Trump himself presents a good case study. His extreme and unique personality traits demonstrate the outer limits of human trait variability. His ego, vanity, ambition, extreme sensitivity to criticism, narcissism, need to dominate and destroy enemies, shamelessness, and desire for acclaim, taken together, are all highly unusual. He differs not only from other members of his family—his sister is a federal judge—but also from most other members of society. Trump built casinos in Atlantic City and amassed his small fortune by exploiting the 2 percent of the population who are problem gamblers. But he's not a problem gambler himself.

How can the same underlying DNA account for such human trait diversity, from extreme risk-takers, introverts, problem gamblers, and egotistical narcissists to psychopaths?

Here's how I would explain it: We humans all have the same traits—interests, motivations, fears, passions, drives, and desires. But those traits are expressed at different intensity levels or thresholds. Some people have high ambition, and some have low ambition. Some people have high social anxiety, and the other 93 percent of the population have lower social anxiety. Some people are introverts, some are extroverts, and so forth.

I never thought I would say this, but Trump is right about one thing: traits remain fairly stable over a lifetime. People don't tend to change from introvert to extrovert or from egotistical narcissist to humanitarian.

We never consciously chose our trait variants. An extrovert doesn't choose to be an extrovert. She simply is that way. Donald Trump never chose to be the way he is. Someone with social anxiety doesn't choose to be that way. It's simply who they are.

Neither do our parents affect our personality trait variants. Trump's father didn't teach him to be a narcissist any more than serial killer Jeffrey Dahmer's father taught him to enjoy necrophilia and cannibalism (Dahmer 1994). The only time we listen to our parents is when—by happy coincidence—we largely agree with what they tell us. Otherwise, as any teenager can tell you, we ignore them.

So if personality trait variations are not assigned by our DNA or genetic differences, or by parents or "society," where do they come from?

Trait Diversity Is Assigned by a Roll of the Dice

I believe that human character trait diversity is allocated by a roll of the "trait assignment dice." By random chance. By lottery. Algorithmically. Not by genetic differences.

What does that mean? Let's use narcissism as an example. Each of us possesses the narcissism trait, but we're randomly assigned a unique narcissism level or threshold, as follows:

```
class NarcissismNeuron:
    def ___init___(self):
        # run this code once when the NarcissismNeuron
        # is first generated in the brain (likely before birth)
        # Assign our narcissism level, by a roll of the dice
        # 0=no narcissism, 100=extreme narcissism
        self.narcissism_level = roll_the_dice(1,100)
```

Everyone has the same `NarcissismNeuron` that implements the trait. When the neuron is first generated in the brain, our narcissism level is set by rolling an internal dice with a value selected randomly between 1 and 100, inclusive. By chance—by luck—Trump was assigned a high narcissism level, probably 99 or 100. For the rest of us, the level averages around 50.

We all have the same traits—caring, obsession, ambition, narcissism, psychopathy, and the like—each implemented by the same algorithms loaded from our shared ancestral DNA library and executed by the same identified neurons.

But each trait comes at a different level, or intensity. I think all our innate—at birth—trait levels are determined post-conception, assigned by a roll of the dice. "Innate" has nothing to do with genetic and DNA variation. The 0.1 percent DNA difference among us is not enough to swap in and out each trait. (I'll concede that in some cases the dice may be slightly rigged to shift the probabilities, such as when traits run in families.)

For example, the prevalence of social anxiety is around 7 percent, but we all share the same `SocialAnxietyNeuron` and its accompanying algorithm or model, as follows:

```
class SocialAnxietyNeuron:
    def ___init___(self):
        # run this code once to set our social anxiety level
        # when the neuron first develops in the brain
        self.anxiety_level = roll_the_dice(1,100)

    def run(self):
        loop forever:
            # determine if we're in a social setting
            c = sendrequest("SocialSettingNeuron", "detect")
            if c == False:
                continue # restart the loop, no anxiety
            f = sendrequest("FamilySettingNeuron", "detect")
            if f == True:
                continue # restart the loop, no anxiety
            elsif self.anxiety_level > 93:
                # enact basic social anxiety behaviors
                sendrequest("SocialSettingNeuron", "avoid")
            else:
                # No anxiety! Party on, Wayne!
            wait(clocktick)
        # repeat loop
```

Rob Vermiller

If, by a roll of the dice, we're assigned a high level of social anxiety (greater than 93 out of 100), then we avoid social settings. It's a highly complex trait. First, we must be able to detect social settings and then trigger a conditional (if–then–else) response. The same algorithm—the same code—can implement different trait levels.

Awe

Awe is an experience of wonder, admiration, reverence, and respect— but also a little bit of fear and dread—that we experience in the face of authority, beauty, fame, status, sublimity, prestige, and great power. Awe reinforces social hierarchies. Low-status individuals feel reverence for high-status individuals or for abstract all-powerful beings like God (Keltner and Haidt 2003).

Ambitious people (or con men) can leverage (or exploit) the credulity of high-awe people (or marks) by adorning themselves with the public signs of status, wealth, and power. Think church cathedrals and ornate rituals but also eponymous buildings, gold toilet seats, personal helicopters, and power ties.

This is how human society scaled up from small hunter-gather societies— where everyone was equal—to large city-states, where the awestruck ceded power to a ruling elite.

Assuming that a single neuron is responsible for our sense of awe:

```
class AweNeuron:
    def ___init___(self):
        # set our awe threshold once, at birth
        self.awe_level = roll_the_dice(1,100)
        # start life with no awesome people around
        self.awesome_people = []

    def run(self):
        loop forever:
            # do we see anyone standing nearby (or on TV)?
            p = sendrequest("PersonalSpaceNeuron", "getperson")
            if self.awe_level > 50:
                s = sendrequest("StatusNeuron", "detect", p)
```

```
        w = sendrequest("WealthNeuron", "detect", p)
        x = sendrequest("PowerNeuron", "detect", p)
        if s or w or x:
            # add them to the list of awesome people
            self.awesome _people.append(p)
        if p in self.awesome _people:
            # demonstrate subservience to
            # the awesome person
            sendrequest("SubservienceNeuron", p)
    wait(clocktick)
    # repeat loop
```

If we're assigned a high awe score—that is, if we're easily swayed by "awesome" people and events—we'll remember the people with high status, wealth, and power. Obviously, the determination of *high status* is culturally specific. Reread the earlier section on "Disgust" for an example of how such determinations can still be innate.

Speaking of disgust, we must fight our intuition that any discussion of innate trait variability is inherently repulsive. We must study the brain as it is, not how we wish it to be.

Shame

Many successful people—especially politicians—are completely shameless. Evolution decided that having a few shameless people around makes society work "better" over the long term, even if such people are very annoying in the short term.

Shameless people can say what they want regardless of gossip, criticism, ostracism, or consequences. To their credit, they can (sometimes) rally the discontented by saying things no one else is willing to say without regret. Sometimes (not often) society requires just such a kick in the pants. Think of it as a corrective control function for gossip—or political correctness—gone wild. Here's the code:

```
class ShameNeuron:
    def ___init ___(self):
        # set our shame level at birth
        self.shame _level = roll _the _dice(1,100)
```

```
def run(self):
   loop forever:
      if self.shame _level > 10:
         # feel the shame, be a normal person
      else:
         # consider, perhaps, a career in politics?
      wait(clocktick)
   # repeat loop
```

Most of us—not all—want to conform to societal or parental expectations. It simply feels better to obey our parents—before adolescence, anyway—and meet the expectations of our peers and society. The sting of gossip, criticism, and shame is too much for us to bear.

However, a shameless person—that is, one with `self.shame _level < 10`—has no such constraints and is willing to do whatever it takes to get ahead. It must be quite liberating not to wear those innate shackles.

Regret

Amazon.com founder Jeff Bezos famously used a "regret minimization framework" when he made the decision to leave a lucrative Wall Street position to form a start-up company in 1994. He wanted to be able to look back at his life when he was eighty years old and not regret having missed the opportunity (Christian and Griffiths 2016).

Everyone has a regret tolerance, assigned by a roll of the dice, as follows:

```
class RegretNeuron:
   def ___init___(self):
      # set our regret tolerance level at birth
      self.regret _tolerance = roll _the _dice(1,100)
```

By chance, Bezos was allocated an extremely low `regret _tolerance`, which was one factor that led to his billion-dollar fortune. It was not the "feeling" of regret that motivated Bezos so much as the algorithm:

```
def run(self):
   loop forever:
      if self.regret _tolerance < 2:
```

```
        # only 1 percent of people take
        # the rare opportunity
        ops = sendrequest("OpportunityNeuron",
        "get rare")
    if ops != False:
        sendrequest("PlannerNeuron",
        "go", ops)
wait(clocktick)
# repeat loop
```

A small fraction of people—1 percent—have an extremely low regret tolerance for missing rare opportunities. The `OpportunityNeuron` can implement either an Upper Confidence Bound algorithm or Gittins index strategy, which is left as an exercise for the reader.

Guilt

Guilt is a painful emotional experience. We feel guilt when we know we've wronged someone or we're responsible for violating a moral or social standard. We obsess about ways to make it right again.

Again, we don't need to worry about the "feeling" of guilt, as that was addressed in a previous section. Let's focus instead on the outcome of guilt—related to remorse—specifically as a way to a change or censor our future behavior to stop further harm.

I'll assume a single neuron in the brain implements situational guilt.

```
class GuiltNeuron:
    def ___init___(self):
        # start life guilt-free
        self.guilt _events = []

    def run(self):
        loop forever:
            for g in self.guilt _events:
                # decompose guilt into level and target
                (guilt _level, guilt _target) = g
                if guilt _level > 50:
                    # plan something to alleviate guilt/remorse
                    # toward the target
```

```
            sendrequest("PlannerNeuron", …) # do something
        wait(clocktick)
    # repeat loop
```

A guilty state—`guilt _level > 50`—offers us a practical inducement to plan some behavior that alleviates the guilt toward the target, such as a parent or someone else we've done wrong.

What Can We Change about Ourselves?

What can we change about ourselves? Not much, according to a leading neuroscientist:

> There is a massive self-help industry devoted to the idea that we can change ourselves—our habits, our behaviors, even our personalities … [There's an] endless supply of books, videos, seminars, and other materials … These suggest that we can learn the habits of highly effective people, and we too will be highly effective. That we can overcome stress, anxiety, negative thoughts, relationship problems, and low self-esteem, manage the anger, boost our mood, achieve the goals we always hope for, and generally become a happier person …

> But the brain is not infinitely malleable … This limits the amount of change we can expect to achieve … There is little evidence to support the idea that we can really change our personality traits … You may be able to learn behavioral strategies that allow you to adapt better to demands of your life, but these are unlikely to change the predispositions themselves …

> The self-help industry is built on an insidious and even slightly poisonous message. (Mitchell 2018)

This is the standard view—the zeitgeist—among many scientists, although it hasn't yet permeated the public consciousness. Science and intuition are at odds, and intuition is winning. Self-help books continue to fly off the bookstore shelves because our common sense tells us (incorrectly) that we can fundamentally change our own traits.

I agree that we can learn strategies to avoid triggering our afflictions and addictions. Alcoholics can try to avoid situations where they might be tempted to take a drink, although alcoholism itself can't be cured. People with social anxiety can avoid social settings by putting themselves in situations that execute their else code instead of their if code, as follows:

```
c = sendrequest("SocialSettingNeuron", "detect")
if c == True:
    # Get outta there, Steve, it's too dangerous!
    sendrequest("SocialSettingNeuron", "avoid")
else:
    # Ahhhhh, that's better!
```

Can we reset the `SocialAnxietyNeuron`'s original `anxiety_level` later in life? In theory, evolution can write our code any way it wants. If it wanted us to be able to reset our anxiety level, then it would have provided the code to do that:

```
def sendrequest(self, requestor, reqtype, parameters):
    # process a request from another neuron
    # to request our anxiety value
    if reqtype == "setvalue":
        new_value = parameters
        self.anxiety_level = new_value
```

But I doubt it. We humans remain fairly stable in our personality traits throughout our lives. Once a resilient person, always a resilient person. Introverts don't turn into extroverts. On the TV show *Bull*, Dr. Jason Bull, a psychologist and trial science expert, helps win court cases by selecting the best jurors to find a defendant not guilty, by targeting jurors with the "right" personality traits to respond to a specific type of evidence or argument. This (cynical) approach wouldn't work unless personality traits varied across the population and remained stable over time.

However, I don't believe in determinism. Our mental simulation—our parallel universe—resonates with reality in ways that are too complex and mystical to predict.

PART 7—SOCIETY AND CULTURE

Specialization

Thousands of years ago, we humans lived in small bands of hunter-gatherers, no more than 150 people in a group. There was no need for specialized roles. If anyone seized power or became abusive, others could quickly overpower and kill him.

In the Middle East, 12,000 years ago in the Fertile Crescent, humans settled down and began to domesticate wheat, barley, other plants, and animals—the beginning of the Agricultural Revolution. Similar stories played out around the world, including in ancient Egypt and the Indus Valley.

By 6500 years ago, the Sumer civilization developed in Mesopotamia at the beginning of the Bronze Age. Settled communities brought greater population densities. Humans evolved to become less violent, which allowed us to live in closer proximity (Wade 2007). Thousands of humans now lived in villages and city-states.

The impact of the Agricultural Revolution—which resulted in large, complex societies—was a greater specialization of roles. Some became farmers, and others made pottery, tools, irrigation systems, and other implements. Through trade, farmers could acquire tools, and trades people could acquire food.

Having a division of labor allowed human society to scale up as modern city-states arose. (However, the life of the agricultural worker was no better than that of earlier hunter-gatherer tribes, where most men died in battle with other tribes.) Agriculture led to food surpluses, yet the quality and diversity of nutrition decreased and the work was backbreaking.

Specialized political roles and the rule of elites emerged to organize and control the masses. Central administrations and hierarchical religious ideologies evolved. In quick succession, written languages and codified laws became commonplace.

Throughout the transformation from hunter-gatherer to modern society with its division of labor, our DNA evolved very little. The human capacity for role diversity must have existed all along.

Division of Labor

We each have a unique set of interests, obsessions, motivations, drives, desires, and passions. It's easiest to see when we observe the extremes— Donald Trump, Albert Einstein, Abraham Lincoln, and even serial killer Jeffrey Dahmer. Exceptions prove the rule that trait diversity is real, even as we all share the same DNA.

Einstein famously preferred to work alone and avoided personal emotional entanglements. Trump is an extremely thin-skinned narcissist who craves the spotlight. Serial killer Jeffrey Dahmer truly enjoyed killing people and eating their flesh, traits that are too complex to be accidental, even though he hated himself for having these obsessions and compulsions.

Having different interests leads to different roles. For example, I have no desire to become a soldier. I'm not interested in demonstrating my bravery, honor, and service, and nobody can force me to be motivated by acts of valor. It's just not who I am. But imagine if no one was motivated to become a soldier. Then we'd all be defenseless against invaders. On the other hand, if everyone wanted to be a soldier, there would be no one left to farm the land, teach students, treat patients, program computers, or construct buildings. We each have different skills and talents resulting from differing passions, interests, and motivations (Dockx 2017).

This diversity of roles—and division of labor—allows society to scale as we each seek out our specific niche and role. Society thrives on this diversity. We can't all be professors or computer programmers or farmers. Humans are specialized actors. The diversity of roles is necessary for long-term human survival, even if this means the exploitation of some for the benefit of others.

Donald Trump and Me

What would happen if Donald Trump and I were locked in a room together? What would we say to each other? Our conversation and actions would likely be driven by our innate traits—needs, desires, motivations, and interests. As with any human interaction, we'd seek to exploit the other to fulfill those needs.

Let's pick five traits: awe, ambition, guilt, shame, and need for approval. Donald Trump and I obviously have different set levels of these traits, assigned by a roll of the "trait assignment dice."

Donald Trump's traits:

    awe level = 60
    ambition level = 100
    guilt level = 0
    shame level = 0
    craves approval level = 100

My traits:

    awe level = 30
    ambition level = 50
    guilt level = 80
    shame level = 60
    craves approval level = 50

Given these traits, let's sketch out a personality profile for each of us:

- Donald Trump is a highly ambitious individual who craves approval—mostly adulation from crowds, not individuals. He feels awe for political power and leverages material wealth—private airplanes, tall buildings carrying his name, gold-plated toilet seats, and so forth—to represent his status. His lack of shame and guilt allows him to say anything necessary to reach his goals, hire and fire people as needed, and exploit others with a clear conscience.
- I, on the other hand, am mildly ambitious, yet I still enjoy approval from family and friends (not crowds). I don't want to deviate too much from social norms for fear of shame and guilt. My awe level is on the low side, so I'm not a groupie or terribly religious. A charismatic figure like Trump can't win me over easily (I hope).

As we stand together in the room, Trump circles me warily. He asks me pointed questions to determine if I'm a political threat to him. (If so, he would immediately demand that I pledge my loyalty to him, and if such a pledge were not immediately forthcoming, he would seek to attack and destroy me.) However, he quickly determines I'm not a political threat, so he relaxes.

I stare in amazement as I realize we both have the same DNA, yet his traits are so different from mine, assigned by chance by a roll of the trait assignment dice.

I observe the confidence on his face as he speaks. Involuntarily and perhaps subconsciously, I feel myself yielding to him during the conversation and getting out of his way. I'm certainly not in awe of him, and I don't like the way he violates social norms, but my strong sense of decorum and politeness—perhaps stemming from my guilt and shame—keeps me from speaking up. I also don't want him to attack me personally, so I try to be nice, even flattering.

Trump and I both enjoy approval and approbation. He asks me what I do, and I tell him. With total conviction on his face, he says how fantastic people like me are. "You really are terrific," he says.

He tries to win me over and impress me with tales of his business and personal conquests, as well as his material wealth, to convert me into a cheering acolyte, a member of his fan club. Despite myself, I feel a sudden rush stemming from his validation and approbation. I forget his long, sordid history, and I stupidly smile. He smiles at my smile. We both win.

But he's the elite in charge. As long as I don't challenge his authority, and as long as I keep applauding him and stroking his ego, he will act as my confident proxy. Such has been the social contract since before the Agricultural Revolution.

Shyness

No one is shy all the time. At home, in a familiar and comfortable family setting, a person who is naturally shy (in a crowded or public setting) can even be outgoing. Shyness requires a context that is salient to the trait.

However, seven in every thousand children have a more extreme condition known as "selective mutism" (SM), a type of social anxiety that renders children absolutely silent in public even when they are normally talkative at home. Children with SM never speak up in class because they can't. Until recently, the condition was known as "elective mutism," which suggests the silence is willful and controlling, and SM was falsely attributed to emotional or physical abuse. "It was seen as a power struggle that manifested as a refusal to speak. Now it is characterized as a failure to speak." (Cole 2006)

Let's rewrite the code for the SocialAnxietyNeuron mentioned earlier. (I apologize for conflating shyness with social anxiety in this example.):

```
class SocialAnxietyNeuron:
    def ___init___(self):
        # run this code once to set our social anxiety level
        # when the neuron first develops in the brain
        # changed from 100 to 1000
        self.anxiety_level = roll_the_dice(1,1000)

    def run(self):
        loop forever:
            # determine if we're in a social setting
```

```
        c = sendrequest("SocialSettingNeuron", "detect")
        if c == False:
            continue # restart the loop, no anxiety
        f = sendrequest("FamilySettingNeuron", "detect")
        if f == True:
            continue # restart the loop, no anxiety
        elsif self.anxiety_level > 993:
            # 7 in 1000 people have selective mutism
            sendrequest("SpeechNeuron", "disable")
        elsif self.anxiety_level > 930:
            # enact basic social anxiety behaviors
            sendrequest("SocialSettingNeuron", "avoid")
        else:
            # No anxiety! Party on, Wayne!
        wait(clocktick)
    # repeat loop
```

This code supports multiple contexts—family or crowd—as well as
multiple shyness modes. In other words, the code is operating normally as
it was (cruelly) designed by evolution to operate.

If we find ourselves in a crowd and our shyness level—which was assigned
at birth by a roll of the trait assignment dice—exceeds the threshold of
993, we suffer from selective mutism and our SpeechNeuron is disabled.

How does the SocialAnxietyNeuron determine we're in a familiar
setting? By delegating to the FamilySettingNeuron, as follows:

```
class FamilySettingNeuron:
    def ___init___(self):
        # begin life clueless about our family members
        self.potential_family = []
        self.actual_family = []

    def run(self):
        loop forever:
            # We see someone nearby. Are they family?
            p = sendrequest("PersonalSpaceNeuron", "getperson")
            if p not in self.actual_family:
                if p not in self.potential_family:
                    self.potential_family.append(p)
                else:
                    # need a trust algorithm here to determine
```

```
                    # whether they're actual family
          wait(clocktick)
     # repeat loop
```

The `FamilySettingNeuron` keeps track of our `actual _family` members. Newborns stare at their caregiver's face (algorithm not shown) and add them to the list of potential family members. Then another algorithm likely kicks in around three months of age, when infants begin to sift through potential family members to determine who is actual family worth clinging to—and not a stranger worth screaming over—perhaps based on frequency of contact or social referencing cues.

Extroverts and Introverts

Anyone who's taken the Myers–Briggs personality assessment knows whether they're an introvert or extrovert. That assessment is commonly given in corporate settings to build diverse teams. Extroverts tend to be motivated by the external world—networking and talking with others—whereas introverts tend to be motivated by their internal world of thoughts, plans, and ideas. After a party, introverts need some alone time to recover their energy, whereas extroverts don't want the party to end.

According to former GE CEO Jack Welch:

> Many introverts stagnate in large organizations … Big companies are constantly looking for people to move across divisions or around the world, and extroverts, by rights or not, appear more prepared for such opportunities … With their charisma and superior verbal skills, [extroverts are] thought to be more 'out front,' able to communicate powerfully and motivate their people, especially during tough times … Extroverts also tend to forge relationships with more ease, another boon in complex hierarchies … Extroverts tend to outshine introverts because early on, their outsize personalities earn them chances to make presentations to higher-ups, always

a good way to accelerate the career-changing process of getting out of the pile. (Welch and Welch 2008)

Reducing this to code, we get the following:

```
class IntrovertExtrovertNeuron:
    def ___init ___(self):
        # set the level once, before we're born
        self.extroversion _level = roll _the _dice(1,100)
```

By chance, by luck, by lottery, by a roll of the dice, some are born introverts and some are born extroverts (with the latter getting all the promotions and the executive salary).

Jack Welch admits there are a few cases of a "reserved, shy, or awkward individual who has risen through the ranks to run something big." But those are rare exceptions. "Charisma ... seems to be inborn. It can't really be trained" (Welch and Welch 2006).

Leaders

Leaders must exude energy, be able to inspire confidence, and be optimistic and comfortable in their own skin. Leadership should be about rallying people and motivating others to support a great cause. A good leader can look us in the eye and convince us to do things we would not otherwise do.

To become a political leader, one must possess extreme ambition—a lust for power, a "fire in the belly." Every day, they must be driven to work hard and be resilient enough to overcome any obstacles. And even with these attributes, they'd probably never reach the goal; too many other people share the same ambition. But with the right motivation, they'd be relentless in the attempt, a force of nature.

For example, Speaker of the U.S. House of Representatives Nancy Pelosi temporarily lost her position yet worked feverishly to regain it:

> [Pelosi went to work] solidifying the support she would need to reclaim the speaker's gavel, working furiously

through the summer to regain the House majority and meeting privately with the left's ascending political star, Rep.-elect Alexandria Ocasio-Cortez (N.Y.). [a.k.a. AOC]

To nail down the votes, Pelosi deployed the same tactics she used multiple times to muscle hard-fought legislation through the House during her prior tenure as speaker— methodically undermining her opposition, tapping a vast network of allies and relying on a grab bag of political favors. (DeBonis and Costa 2018)

Let's assume we're all born with the same `AmbitionNeuron`, with an `ambition_level` that's established at or around birth, when the neuron is first generated in the brain. The code might look something like this:

```
class AmbitionNeuron:
    def __init__(self):
        # set the level once, before we're born
        self.ambition_level = roll_the_dice(1,100)

    def run(self):
        loop forever:
            if self.ambition_level > 90:
                sendrequest("BefriendPowerfulPeopleNeuron", True)
                sendrequest("VanquishCriticsNeuron", True)
                sendrequest("SeekAcclaimNeuron", True)
                sendrequest("CraveApplauseNeuron", True)
                sendrequest("BuildAlliancesNeuron", True)
            wait(clocktick)
        # repeat loop
```

Our `ambition_level` is chosen randomly, by a roll of the trait assignment dice. If the level exceeds a certain threshold, we demonstrate ambition behaviors. Same code, different outcome. Our ambition level defines who we are and guides our choices in life. Some people have ambition, and some people don't.

Ambition and charisma don't always go hand in hand (think Richard Nixon). But when they do, a rare charismatic leader emerges. Such leaders don't require approval or approbation to feel self-confident. They are convinced by the righteousness of their cause, and they have no internal conflicts. They can laugh enthusiastically, promote new ideas, and infect others with their optimism. They're self-confident and emotionally expressive. Former president Bill Clinton was famously energized by crowds, but he was needy too. Politicians want us to like them (Dockx 2017).

Every human has in his or her brain a neuron that executes the charisma program. The program runs normally regardless of our ambition level. It looks like this:

```
class CharismaNeuron:
    def ___init___(self):
        # set the level once, before we're born
        self.charisma_level = roll_the_dice(1,100)

    def run(self):
        loop forever:
            if self.charisma_level > 90:
                # exude energy, inspire confidence
                # be optimistic
                # be comfortable in own skin
                # yada yada
            wait(clocktick)
        # repeat loop
```

It's not easy to dream up the rest of the algorithm for charisma. If we were trying to write the code for a charismatic robot instead of a human, what would that code look like? An easy smile, free of constraints. That's not too hard. Optimistic; comfortable in their own metallic skin; ability to rally and motivate people. Again, I'll leave this as an exercise for the reader for extra credit!

Followers

High-status individuals—as indicated by their confidence, position, possessions, or behavior—can be very attractive. When we see someone demonstrate extreme vanity, instead of being turned off, we often believe they must be important because they value themselves so highly. If someone speaks with absolute confidence, others will be convinced they're the boss.

If they flaunt their wealth, expensive cars and houses, and gold-plated toilet seats, many will assume they have high status.

As followers, we want to identify with the emotions of high-status leaders. We want to please them and receive their approbation and approval in return. Leadership is transactional. We followers are happy when our leader is happy and sad when they're sad. That's the nature of being a follower. If our leader is abusive toward us, we feel stress and dismay, but we also feel more motivated to please him or her in the future.

> Steve Jobs, the CEO of Apple, charmed and attracted new talent with his vision of the future—often referred to as his "reality distortion field"—after which he was often abusive to those same employees, paying them poorly, taking credit for their work, and shunning them, even after many years of service, if they were critical or disloyal in any way. Yet computer engineers willingly worked ninety-hour weeks on his behalf.
>
> In the early 1960s, Yale University psychologist Stanley Milgram ran a study in which volunteers were told by a lab technician—an authority figure—to punish a subject with an electric shock every time he made a mistake on a test. No electric shock was actually given, although the volunteers didn't know that. They were ordered by the technician to increase the voltage, even after the subject cried out in pain, to levels they were told would kill the subject. Although under stress, the volunteers complied rather than defy the authority figure.
>
> And remember Jonestown? A cult leader named Jim Jones ordered his fanatical followers to drink from a vat of Kool-Aid laced with cyanide. Most willingly complied, and 918 of his followers died that day. They trusted their leader to the end. (Dockx 2017)

Most of us are evolutionarily wired to be followers—to drink the Kool-Aid. Unfortunately, we humans are all too easily exploited by a zealot or charlatan or con man. We're hardwired to trust someone who is confident and appears convinced by what they are saying. We want to believe.

Fortunately for leaders, most of us want to follow. We seek validation from those in authority. We feel awe for their status and power. Extreme traits like social anxiety also keep followers in line, which allows leaders to establish dominance hierarchies that allow society to scale. I wish it were not so.

By my theory, we each possess a single `FollowerNeuron`:

```
class FollowerNeuron:
    def ___init___(self):
        # set the level once, before we're born
        self.followership_level = roll_the_dice(1,100)

    def run(self):
        loop forever:
            p = sendrequest("PersonalSpaceNeuron", "getperson")
            s = sendrequest("StatusNeuron", "detect", p)
            if s == True and self.followership_level > 30
                sendrequest("SubmissiveBehaviorNeuron", "go", p)
            wait(clocktick)
        # repeat loop
```

If our `followership_level` is randomly assigned to be greater than 30, and if we detect a high-status individual or leader nearby, we'll trigger our `SubmissiveBehaviorNeuron`. It's just who we are.

The reality is more complicated, of course. High-status individuals fill socially and culturally defined roles and positions. When they lose their position, they lose status in our eyes, and we treat them differently. As with chickens, the pecking order keeps changing. The code must keep track, not only of who's up and who's down but also of their respective positions in the hierarchy.

Psychopaths

The phrase "he's an assassin" is considered a compliment, used to describe many successful entrepreneurs and business leaders. It implies laser focus, steely nerves, ice water in the veins, and clear-minded decision-making prowess.

Most of us are held back by our "normal" traits: a natural sense of shame, embarrassment, modesty, and guilt, randomly allocated by the trait assignment dice. But an assassin-like business leader, shameless politician, or demagogue lacks these shackles and thus possesses a greater ability to achieve business goals and success by climbing the ladders of power.

Psychopaths have an even greater advantage (Babiak and Hare 2006). It turns out that many psychopaths are successful businesspeople. In the workplace, they can be charming and manipulative and single-minded. Psychopaths don't feel shame or guilt. They are able to break human bonds quickly, such as when firing or laying off staff. In war, psychopaths don't feel PTSD; they just keep on fighting. In ancient battles with Neanderthals, their ability to carry on despite adversity must have been highly prized.

Psychopathic traits are so complex—ability to charm others; grandiose sense of self; cunning, callous, and manipulative behavior—that a substantial amount of neural programming is required to implement the trait. Psychopathy is no accident or mistake from an evolutionary standpoint. Because we all share the same DNA, everyone must have a `PsychopathNeuron` in the brain.

The prevalence of psychopathy in the population is 1 percent. This ratio was found to be "just right" by the process of evolution for the long-term survival of the human species, the same way a single drop of sriracha hot sauce is all that's needed to spice up a bowl of noodle soup. Having this many psychopaths around must benefit society somehow, perhaps by introducing radical new ideas or leading people in dramatic new directions. Just as often, however, the outcome is malevolent and violent and oppressive, as human history will attest.

The PsychopathNeuron switches off other traits such as shame, guilt, and modesty and turns up the volume on other traits like ambition (which contradicts my earlier claim that trait levels can't really be changed. Hmm, perhaps there is hope after all!):

```
class PsychopathNeuron:
    def ___init___(self):
        p = roll_the_dice(1,100)
        # let's make the trait all or nothing
        # we have a 1% chance of being a psychopath
        if p == 100:
            self.psychopath = True
        else:
            self.psychopath = False

    def run(self):
        loop forever:
            if self.psychopath == True:
                sendrequest("ShameNeuron","setvalue",0)
                sendrequest("GuiltNeuron","setvalue",0)
                sendrequest("ModestyNeuron","setvalue",0)
                sendrequest("AmbitionNeuron","setvalue",100)
            else:
                # congratulations, you're not a psychopath!
            wait(clocktick)
        # repeat loop
```

In this example, psychopathy is an all-or-nothing trait. If we exceed the threshold—by a roll of the dice—then we're 100 percent psychopath. Otherwise, we're 0 percent psychopath. Same code, different outcome. Starting from childhood.

> A nine-year-old boy named Jeffrey Bailey pushed a toddler into the deep end of a motel swimming pool in Florida. As the boy struggled and sank to the bottom, Bailey pushed up a chair to watch. Questioned by the police afterward, Bailey explained that he was curious to see someone drown. When he was taken into custody, he seemed untroubled by the prospect of jail but was pleased to be the center of attention. (Kahn 2012)

Examining the extremes is useful to illustrate what is possible, and what must be explained, by any theory of mind. We all have the same DNA. If even one person has a trait, then it must lie dormant in all of us.

The Dark Side of Human Nature

We humans clearly have a dark side. Psychologists have found that we secretly—and perhaps subconsciously—believe many nasty things that we would never admit publicly (Jarrett 2018). We often view minorities and the vulnerable as less than human. We assume that the downtrodden of the world deserve their fate. We experience Schadenfreude (pleasure at another person's distress) by the age of four. We attribute other people's bad deeds, such as our partner's infidelities, to their character while attributing the same deeds performed by ourselves to the situation at hand. We are sexually attracted to people with dark personality traits including narcissism, psychopathy, and Machiavellianism. We favor ineffective leaders with psychopathic traits.

You may protest: "That's not me! I'm not like that!" Okay, fine. The hardest part about programming the brain is facing up to who we really are, warts and all. Like it or not, the algorithm for each of these characteristics must lay hidden in our collective human DNA, implemented by identified neurons. If we're in denial, we can't write the code.

Fortunately, culture and society can counteract—in a top-down causal (TDC) manner—our worst impulses. If we see poor people or immigrants, our gut feeling may be a mixture of both pity and disgust. But if our leaders implore us to take pity, we forget our disgust. On the other hand, if our chosen leaders validate and exploit our sense of disgust for political purposes, we forget our pity.

PART 8—PREPARING FOR THE ROBOTS

A New Politics Is Needed

Before society is ready for the coming age of intelligent robots and the resulting displacement of many jobs through automation, we've got to get our politics right.

Today, politics has become very polarized. Narrowcast news outlets and social media groups cater to small, like-minded communities in a giant echo chamber. Republicans (i.e., conservatives, the Right) only talk to their friends, and Democrats (i.e., liberals, the Left) only talk to their friends, and never the two shall meet. Both sides watch TV shows and listen to internet podcasts that reinforce and validate their existing beliefs. It's comforting for Republicans to listen to Fox News, and Democrats feel equally comforted by commentary provided by a variety of other news outlets, like NPR, MSNBC, and CNN, that reflect their thinking. No one is particularly interested in understanding the perspective of the other side.

With the egregious practice of gerrymandering congressional districts whereby one district is configured to be mostly Democratic and another mostly Republican, with the goal of "wasting" the votes above 50 percent in winner-take-all elections, politicians are becoming more radical. Politicians get elected by catering only to their base—one extreme constituency or the other, Right or Left.

111

Nobody is born a Republican or Democrat, of course. Our culture simply provides these as the primary options for political affiliation. As individuals, we sit back and observe the platforms and rhetoric of both major political parties to see what resonates with our interests. We tend to join the party that best matches our beliefs. When we're young, we may follow our parents' political affiliations, but after our teenage years, we tend to forge our own identity and political path.

The raw material of political affiliation is the "moral intuitions" that are hardwired into our brain (Keltner and Haidt 2003). We're all born with a sense of awe, fairness, and group loyalty; respect for authority; and disgust for the impure (or not). But, as we've seen, the level or intensity of these intuitions differs among us, with the variation allocated by random chance. Not everyone has the same threshold of awe, respect for authority, or disgust.

So let's divide society roughly into two groups having different moral intuitions:

- Group A members have a high level of interest in loyalty, respect for authority, purity/sanctity (very sensitive to disgust), liberty, and awe.
- Group B members have a high level of interest in care, justice, and equality/fairness but a lower level of interest in loyalty, respect for authority, purity/sanctity, liberty, and awe.

People in group A look around and are attracted to the Republican Party, which resonates with their interests, needs, motivations, and desires. People in group B also look around and are attracted to the Democratic Party. We seek to join a group of like-minded others whose beliefs resonate with our own subconscious interests and biases.

Republicans believe in individual liberty. They say we deserve to keep what we make by way of our own merit and hard work. There's no such thing as luck. Republicans believe we should respect authority figures like politicians and business and religious leaders. Conservative republicanism is rooted in morality, right and wrong, law and order, individual responsibility, personal agency, and self-reliance. We make our choices freely. It must be so; otherwise, we can't hold others accountable for their actions, the whole basis for the legal system. Conservatives believe that people with natural gifts should be free to succeed, and if they make vast amounts of money, so be it—they deserve it. They worked hard for it.

Democrats, on the other hand, believe in equality of outcomes. They want a more equitable society even if means higher taxes on the rich to support the poor. They believe that the weak should be supported by the government. Luck plays a big part in life, especially for those born into wealthy families or who get lucky breaks like being born a white male in a society that discriminates against minorities and women. The social safety net should be funded by the redistribution of wealth from the lucky rich to the unlucky poor. It's only fair and just, they say. Liberal democratic beliefs are rooted in compassion, freedom of expression, and "I am my brother's keeper." Those interested in support for the downtrodden and who have a belief in human dignity are drawn to the liberals. People are poor because of discrimination or bad luck, they say, and they dismiss any talk of innateness. People are infinitely malleable in their character traits!

Once we've found a party to join—Republican or Democrat—other traits kick in. We become more extreme and territorial. We feel the need to demonstrate our wholehearted loyalty to the group. We must commit—all in—to *all* our group's beliefs. To fit in, we must demonstrate "other hatred" for the other political group. We must become an advocate, even a proselytizer for our group, even if we don't agree with everything they say. The party exerts a top-down causal influence over our behavior. If we should fail to demonstrate enough enthusiasm, our group may reject us, perhaps our greatest fear.

I think both parties have it wrong.

Republicans are wrong to believe that we are personally responsible for our traits and that we deserve to keep all the money we make. Clearly there is a big element of luck involved (Gromet, Hartson and Sherman 2015). Democrats are wrong to believe that humans are infinitely malleable and that we have no innate traits. As we've seen, trait differences are clearly innate and allocated by luck—a roll of the dice.

So what to do about it?

> The philosopher John Rawls proposed that "justice is fairness" (Rawls 1971). He stated that we should establish the rules of society under a "veil of ignorance" over what our future position in that society may be. If we don't know ahead of time our social status or "distribution of natural assets and abilities," Rawls said we'd probably design a government and society that would give us the best life under every possible scenario in which we could be born—rich or poor, advantaged or disadvantaged. Everyone would enjoy basic liberties, inequality of distribution of resources could be tolerated if it would benefit everyone, and opportunities should be open to all people with merit. Everyone would have a fair chance to develop the skills they needed to attain merit. (Dockx 2017)

But to achieve this is not so easy. I think we need a new political party that can acknowledge and reconcile the truth before we plunge ahead with the coming age of robotics and intelligent automation. Politics and AI will become one.

Free Will and Personal Responsibility

Free will has been hotly debated for thousands of years. Aristotle, for example, defined free will as the freedom to do what we want without outside interference. This is probably the common sense view of free will.

The philosopher Arthur Schopenhauer said that "Man can do what he wills but he cannot will what he wills" (Schopenhauer 1839). In other words, we can choose to do what we want, but we're not free to choose our wants themselves. Our wants define us. A non-narcissist can't choose to be motivated by Trumpian narcissism. An introvert can't choose to be motivated by those things that motivate an extrovert. An alcoholic can't choose not to be tempted by alcohol (although he can try to limit his opportunities for temptation).

For a narcissist, it's just who they are. It's part of their identity as a person, and they wouldn't want to be any other way. They choose their narcissistic behavior of their own free will, the same way an elevator chooses to go up and down, because that's what it's designed to do. If they were to lose their narcissism, they would be a different person in some respects. But they are never free in their choice to be a narcissist in the first place.

At some level, we're not responsible for the traits we received by a roll of the algorithmic trait assignment dice—post-conception, before birth, as our neurons came online—because we never consciously selected them, even though those traits define us. A psychopath is not responsible for receiving the psychopathic trait, even though she is defined by her psychopathy. She exercises free will—in the Aristotelean sense—when she acts on her trait. She's simply doing what she wants to do.

Once our trait levels are assigned, the decisions made by those traits—by identified neurons—simply bubble up from our subconscious. We decide to smile or to drink a glass of water before we are consciously aware of our choice. Subconscious brain activity precedes conscious awareness by half a second (Libet, et al. 1983).

That's not to say we humans are deterministic robots. We have many competing desires, and our traits are in constant competition with each other. With quantum uncertainty, unpredictable sensory inputs, top-down causality (TDC), and the impossibility of tracking every particle in the universe to establish an unbroken chain of causes and effects, determinism is a pretty silly position to take.

However, free will is a different issue. We don't make our choices consciously, and we never chose the trait levels that lead to the choices— they are assigned to us by a roll of the dice. So, the only free will we have is to (subconsciously) choose the things we (by the trait assignment dice) want to do.

Personal responsibility, then, becomes more of a social and cultural belief or artifact. As members of a society, we agree to live within a system of beliefs, which then exert TDC on our behavior. We have faith in our beliefs, which bind us together as a group. There's nothing necessarily wrong with that. But beliefs do have consequences.

The Role of Luck

If it's true that trait variation is assigned by a roll of the dice, then it follows that our success in life (or lack thereof) is partly due to luck. Our traits—motivations, interests, desires, passions, fears, drives—determine how we spend our time, what we learn, and which talents we develop. Time on task leads to skill and then to expertise. If making money is our passion—assigned by a roll of the dice—we become good at it. Jobs in the financial industry pay very well. If, on the other hand, we're motivated by caring for others, the available jobs are often lower paid. There is a direct correlation between the outcome of the trait assignment dice and income inequality.

Liberals tend to believe that success comes from luck (Gromet, Hartson and Sherman 2015), whereas conservatives believe it stems from merit (Frank 2016). Conservatives believe this in their guts, so no amount of rational argument will convince them otherwise. It's not a rational thing.

> Conservatives [are] less supportive of the notion that luck is influential to success because the randomness it invokes challenges their belief that people's outcomes are deserved, whereas the notion of random chance contributing to success is consistent with the liberal worldview. (Keltner and Haidt 2003)

It makes sense, then, that liberals and progressives disagree on the role of government. Liberals believe the government should rectify inequality in outcomes because nobody should be held responsible for their bad luck in life. Conservatives believe in personal responsibility, liberty, merit, and initiative—no luck about it. To their credit, conservatives have a healthy skepticism about what often corrupt governments can actually accomplish.

I think that if you're lucky, you bear only a limited responsibility for the resulting traits and outcomes, positive or negative.

Universal Basic Income (UBI)

In Germany, the automotive industry employs around a million people, many of them non-college-educated. Like in the United States in the 1950s, the German middle class feels empowered and appreciated. They have a sense of purpose. Income inequality is steadily rising, but it has not yet led to widespread social unrest, as it did earlier in the twentieth century with disastrous consequences.

That is all about to change, however. The auto industry is shifting to electric cars, which require fewer non-college-educated workers to manufacture. Self-driving cars and taxis will eventually reduce automobile ownership and transportation jobs. The entire industry will soon be radically restructured. The plentiful jobs currently available for non-college-educated workers will disappear. With the resulting unemployment, social unrest will soon follow.

In the United States, the day of reckoning has already arrived according to presidential candidate Andrew Yang:

> Between 2.2 and 3.1 million car, bus, and truck driving jobs in the United States will be eliminated by the advent of self-driving vehicles ... Automation has already eliminated about 4 million manufacturing jobs in the United States since 2000 ... The U.S. labor force participation rate is now at only 62.9 percent, a rate below that of nearly all other industrialized economies.

> The normal American did not graduate from college and doesn't have an associate's degree ... She or he has a net worth of approximately $36K ... and lives paycheck to paycheck ... [A] Federal Reserve report in 2015 said that 75 percent of Americans could not pay a $400 emergency expense out of their checking or saving accounts ...

Donald Trump's election in late 2016 … felt like a cry for help.

The logic of the meritocracy is leading us to ruin because we are collectively primed to ignore the voices of the millions getting pushed into economic distress by the grinding wheels of automation and innovation. (Yang 2018)

Yang suggests that the government should offer a universal basic income (UBI)—$1,000 a month—to all adult citizens, paid for by a value-added tax (VAT), to ease the transition and job displacements. If no one has cash to spend, who will buy the output of robot-filled factories or hail a self-driving taxi? The economy would grind to a halt.

But UBI is not the only answer. We must also reinvent human purpose. What gives life meaning when a robot takes your job? Certainly not sitting home doing nothing and collecting a paycheck. The opioid epidemic is proof that humans fall apart without stimulation, validation, and purpose and will seek any path to happiness and fulfilment, even if it's temporary and self-destructive.

Redefining Capitalism

The need to address inequality in outcomes is not a call for the return of socialism and communism. Central economic planning and collective ownership of the means of production are discredited and dysfunctional systems prone to corruption, abuse, and trampling of personal freedoms. Human nature is ugly, and greedy and ambitious central planners will always seize power if they're allowed to.

Capitalism is a highly efficient system for delivering goods and services and inventing new product ideas. Capitalism is responsible for our way of life. Disease and poverty have greatly decreased in the past hundred years. The profit motive is very strong for entrepreneurs, and their outputs—new antibiotics, new labor-saving devices—benefit society as a whole. Even venture capital—large pools of centralized wealth that can be risked on new innovations—is an important part of capitalism.

That said, social programs in a well-run capitalist and democratic society are the best way to address inequality of outcomes:

> Some progressive U.S. politicians now describe themselves as socialists, and a significant number of voters, including a majority of voters under 30, say they approve of socialism. But neither the politicians nor the voters are clamoring for government seizure of the means of production ...

> What Americans who support "socialism" actually want is what the rest of the world calls social democracy: A market economy, but with extreme hardship limited by a strong social safety net and extreme inequality limited by progressive taxation. They want us to look like Denmark or Norway, not Venezuela ...

> [American] voters overwhelmingly support most of the policies proposed by American "socialists," including higher taxes on the wealthy and making Medicare available to everyone. (Krugman 2019)

I think anyone should be free to own and trade large assets, including stock in multibillion-dollar corporations. But nobody deserves to take home a massive income or capital gain if it's merely the outcome of good fortune. (By income, I mean any source of funds that can be used to buy a personal discretionary item like a car, house, or microwave.) Keep your money in your assets, not in your pocket!

To address income inequality, a progressive or VAT tax on the not fully deserving lucky, a universal basic income and shared social programs, and a renewed sense of purpose are clearly needed and justified.

Meaning and Purpose

What's the meaning of life? That's an easy one: "every day, have a purpose." It may be serving others. It may be furthering your own personal ambition. It may be reaching a short-term goal. It may be a making a scientific breakthrough or achieving world peace. Or it may simply be gaining social acceptance and validation.

Society and culture give us meaning and purpose. We all have the same basic set of underlying interests, desires, and motivations defined in our collective DNA. But these traits can be reconfigured by our group beliefs the way balls can settle into different stable configurations inside a bag. Society and culture give us purpose and provide an environment—a context—for our emotions and the mental traits to seek engagement, validation, and fulfillment.

Culture provides a context in which our brains, and specifically our neurons, behave. We're hardwired in our neural programming with the hooks to allow culture to affect us. We feel shame—at least most of us do—when we violate cultural norms. We feel guilt—at least most of us do—when we receive more than others do. We feel indignant—at least most of us do—when someone cuts in front of us in line. We enjoy meeting societal or parental expectations, and we feel stress and guilt when we don't.

The rules of society and culture impose top-down causality (TDC) on individual human behavior and provide a set of guiderails and constraints that allow society to organize and scale. These rules define the set of shared beliefs and myths we live by, and these beliefs have a top-down effect on our behavior that both binds and frees us.

For example, in the US military, a core belief is that "no man is left behind" in battle. It's inconvenient, and often deadly, to rescue fallen soldiers in enemy territory. But the result of the belief is that our behavior is changed. Captured soldiers know they will be rescued, so they don't easily give up their secrets.

Cultural belief in free will also changes our behavior. We believe we freely make our own choices; otherwise, we can't hold each other accountable for our actions. We believe in the concepts of liberty and equality because our group finds them important. We believe leaders should be elected to serve for a finite period of time and then step aside. Chimpanzee societies are ruled by alpha males, but we believe in rule of law, not rule of alpha males. We believe in human rights, freedom of speech, and moral equality. Every life has equal moral worth. Why? Can it be logically proven? No. Is it actually true that every human life has equal moral worth the same way that 1 + 1 = 2 is true? As a member of our liberal democracy, I would have to say yes. My belief is the price of group membership. If enough people believe something, it changes our behavior and our culture. It becomes a self-fulfilling prophecy, for good or ill.

Sociocultural beliefs and norms are both powerful and extremely dangerous. Most (not all) humans are vulnerable, primed with traits like awe, respect for authority, modesty, shame, followership, and a need for social acceptance. Specialized actors in society (politicians, leaders) know how to exploit these traits for their own purposes. Good leaders gently corral us, convince us, charm us, build coalitions of the willing, and guide our better nature to positive ends. But demagogues, charlatans, cult leaders, and zealots seek only to incite our ancient fears and cravings for strong leadership, and they turn us against one another to further their own autocratic power and increase their wealth.

In our quest for meaning, we must remain vigilant and watchful for charismatic robots.

AR Attaboy

How will we find meaning and purpose in our lives when our jobs are replaced by robots and intelligent automation?

Perhaps augmented reality (AR) can help. AR will soon be pervasive. By wearing special glasses, we can superimpose imaginary artifacts onto our own reality. The most important of these artifacts will be other people, even artificial ones.

We're social beings. Most of us crave to be around others IRL (in real life). We crave interaction, approbation, and being useful to give us purpose. Being surrounded by artificial life-forms in AR will seem odd at first. But children and young adults are already "digitally native" and comfortable playing games like Fortnite, Minecraft and Pokémon GO in 3-D worlds filled with imaginary characters. They'll catch on quickly.

Snapchat filters that alter our faces by drawing on a funny mustache are just the beginning of AR, even as technical challenges remain. An artificial character sitting at our dinner table or walking around in our house must maintain contact with the ground (obey the rules of gravity), avoid obstacles, and partly disappear when occluded behind a couch.

Interacting with AR characters is another matter. Adding physical interactivity—touch—will be a challenge. Asking them questions and having them respond is still a research problem, although voice recognition, speech-to-text, and chatbot technologies have greatly improved. Perhaps at first we can just tell them what to say ("Tell me I look marvelous today") or use them as avatars to talk to real people around the world.

But it's hard to overstate the power of seeing another person—even a virtual one—in our room, especially if we live alone. With utter conviction—even charisma—on their face, they can smile at us, say "Attaboy!" and tell us how great and important we are to them. They can give us small (virtual) tasks to perform and praise us when we complete them. We can feel rewarded, validated, and self-actualized under the glow of their (virtual) attention. True AI is the ability to convince us we're special.

A politician who craves acclaim might summon a different AR scenario. Standing in an empty auditorium, he or she would pull up a simulation that superimposes a large crowd gazing up at him or her with adoring smiles, wildly applauding.

I believe immersive AR—like the VR in the movie *Ready Player One*—could be used to alleviate widespread dissatisfaction with one's role in the future, albeit imperfectly. Not everyone wants to be an information worker or computer programmer. Many service jobs—taxi and truck driver, fast-food worker, factory worker—will be replaced by intelligent robots, stoking anger and frustration. Even if the government guarantees a basic income, we want to find fulfillment in our work. I predict—although I wish it could be otherwise—that AR will provide a sense of meaning and purpose to millions of the displaced in the future.

You might find it a sad outcome, like a dystopian episode of *Dark Mirror*. But the future is very difficult to predict. Twenty years ago, nobody predicted we would all spend so much time staring at our mobile phones. Had they known, they would have protested. But now it's normal. In less than a hundred years, it's possible that we'll all transfer our minds into robot bodies. You can complain now if you'd like. By then it will be normal.

Yet AR won't arrive unless it appears credible, and credibility requires true artificial intelligence.

Artificial General Intelligence (AGI)

In the movie *Ex Machina*, a robot, Ava, learns to outmaneuver and manipulate humans and trick them into believing she has humanlike intelligence and emotions. Does this make her "artificially intelligent"? Yes, I think so. If a robot is sophisticated enough to deeply mirror the internal emotional state of others and manipulate and outsmart them, she must be intelligent.

Today's understanding of artificial intelligence (AI) and deep-learning neural networks is sufficient to solve narrowly defined problems, like self-driving cars, speech-to-text conversion, sophisticated data analytics, and playing chess. That's all very impressive. Computers now regularly defeat the human world chess champion, and we're on the cusp of replacing truck drivers with self-driving trucks.

But AI is still extremely fragile, relying mostly on sophisticated pattern recognition. Although the brain might employ such techniques for specific applications, current AI does not mimic how the brain works in general. We humans can easily learn new concepts, comprehend complex ideas, generalize principles from specific examples, think abstractly, and infer cause and effect. We can plan for the future and learn from the past. AI can't do any of that. Perhaps reassuringly, Ava can't be built using AI technology the way it's defined today, although initiatives like OpenAI are currently pursuing new approaches to artificial general intelligence (AGI).

In this book, I've described a new and sometimes fanciful theory of how I believe the brain really works, at least conceptually. Identified neurons are the primary actors (agents) in the brain. They're like little independent computers, each with a unique name or address. They load and execute their algorithms from our shared human DNA library and communicate with other neurons via messages to accomplish their goals and objectives. Memories are stored locally in identified neurons as DNA recordings. Each of the 100 billion neurons in the human brain jealously fights for its own agenda and resources and trusts others do the same.

I propose that each human trait—motivation, fear, desire, passion—is implemented by a single, identified neuron. All humans—having the same DNA—have the same set of identified neurons and thus the same trait algorithms. We each perceive the world the same way to allow our shared trait algorithms to process and respond to our shared experiences.

The mind—a.k.a. parallel universe or simulation—emerges from the activity of billions of individual, self-interested neurons, sometimes competing, sometimes cooperating. The mind's parallel universe, tightly synchronized with reality, allows us to move backward and forward in time and space, to consider the future and reflect on the past.

Consciousness is merely our current location in the mental simulation. Our choices and decisions are largely subconscious, made by locally by empowered, identified neurons. However, the harmonies and resonant frequencies arising in the brain from the interaction of neural agents, and the expectations of society and culture, exert a powerful top-down causal influence on our neurons and behavior.

The "feeling" of happiness, sadness, pain, and the like arises from dissonances and perturbations in the parallel universe and the resulting constraints on our actions. With "feeling" thus explained, I was able to ignore it and consider traits and emotions algorithmically, in terms of their inputs and outputs.

All humans have the same traits, even pathological ones, but trait levels or intensities are assigned by a roll of the dice—by chance, by lottery, by luck. (I don't believe genetic differences lead to trait variations; instead, trait diversity is assigned by an algorithm, outside our control.) Since our trait levels are randomly assigned to us, we're not fully responsible for the outcome. Trait diversity allows society to scale even as the resulting division of labor leads to inequality that should be rectified.

Philosophically, neither of the major political parties thinks about humans this way. Society and culture thus require a new set of beliefs and myths. We need a new politics for the age of robots and intelligent automation, one based on a new understanding of personal responsibility, fairness, and the role of luck in outcomes. We need to reestablish human dignity, purpose, and meaning—perhaps using augmented reality—for a time when our labor is no longer needed.

Using the tools and techniques described in this book, we could, I believe, successfully program an intelligent robot like Ava or even transfer our own minds to robot bodies and program ourselves. [Whoever cracks the code first will be celebrated as the next Einstein, and true AI will arrive a year or two after that.] Should we do it? You now have the tools. Decide for yourself.

REFERENCES

Abar, S, G Theodoropoulos, P Lemarinier, and G O'Hare. 2017. "Agent Based Modelling and Simulation tools: A review of the state-of-art software." *Computer Science Review* Volume 24, Pages 13-33. doi:10.1016/j.cosrev.2017.03.001.

Babiak, P. 1995. "When Psychopaths go to Work: A Case Study of an Industrial Psychopath." *Applied Psychology* vol. 44, no. 2, pp. 171 – 188.

Babiak, P, and R Hare. 2006. *Snakes in Suits: When Psychopaths go to Work.* HarperCollins.

Balter, M. 2000. "Was Lamarck Just a Little Bit Right?" *Science* 288 (5463): 38. doi:10.1126/science.288.5463.38.

Bandura, A. 1997. *Self-Efficacy: The Exercise of Control.* Macmillan.

Barford, E. 2013. *Nature News.* Sept 18. https://www.nature.com/news/parasite-makes-mice-lose-fear-of-cats-permanently-1.13777.

Barkow, J, L Cosmides, and J Tooby. 1992. *The Adapted mind: evolutionary psychology and the generation of culture.* Oxford Univ Press.

Bédécarrats, A, S Chen, K Pearce, D Cai, and D Glanzman. 2018. "RNA from Trained Aplysia Can Induce an Epigenetic Engram for Long-Term Sensitization in Untrained Aplysia." *eNeuro.* doi:10.1523/ENEURO.0038-18.2018.

Bird, S, E Klein, and E Loper. 2009. *Natural Language Processing with Python.* O'Reilly Media, Inc.

Blackiston, D, E Silva Casey, and M Weiss. 2008. "Retention of Memory through Metamorphosis: Can a Moth Remember What It Learned As a Caterpillar?" *PLOS ONE.* doi:10.1371/journal.pone.0001736.

Bloom, P. 2013. *Just babies: The origins of good and evil.* New York: Crown Publishers/Random House.

Boldrini, M. 2018. "Human Hippocampal Neurogenesis Persists throughout Aging." *Cell Stem Cell.* doi:10.1016/j.stem.2018.03.015.

Bowers, JS. 2009. "On the biological plausibility of grandmother cells. Implications for neural network theories in psychology and neuroscience." *Psychological Review* 116 (1): 220–251. doi:10.1037/a0014462.

Buonomano, D. 2017. *Your Brain is a Time Machine: The Neuroscience and Physics of Time.* W. W. Norton & Company.

Campbell, J. 2014. *The Hero's Journey: Joseph Campbell on His Life and Work.* New World Library.

Carey, S. 2009. *The Origin of Concepts.* Oxford University Press, Inc.

Cepelewicz, J. 2016. "The U.S. Government Launches a $100-Million "Apollo Project of the Brain"." *Scientific American,* Mar 8. https://www.scientificamerican.com/article/the-u-s-government-launches-a-100-million-apollo-project-of-the-brain/.

Chomsky, N. 1957. *Syntactic Structures.* The Hague/Paris: Mouton, ISBN 978-3-11-021832-9.

Christian, B, and T Griffiths. 2016. *Algorithms to live by: The computer science of human decisions.* New York: Henry Holt and Company, LLC.

Clark, A. 2008. *Supersizing the Mind: Embodiment, Action, and Cognitive Extension.* Oxford University Press.

Cole, W. 2006. "Why Abby Won't Talk." *Time,* Jan 29.

Dahmer, L. 1994. *A Father's Story.* William Morrow and Company, Inc.

Darwin, Charles. 1872. *The expression of the emotions in man.* John Murray.

DeBonis, M, and R Costa. 2018. "'Her skills are real': How Pelosi put down a Democratic rebellion in bid for speaker." *Washington Post,* Dec 13. https://www.washingtonpost.com/powerpost/her-skills-are-real-how-pelosi-put-down-a-democratic-rebellion-in-bid-for-speaker/2018/12/13/27bbc7c6-fefa-11e8-ad40-cdfd0e0dd65a_story.html.

Dockx, A. 2017. *A Theory of Inequality.*

Dreberab, A, and C Apicellac. 2009. "The 7R polymorphism in the dopamine receptor D4 gene (DRD4) is associated with financial risk taking in men." *Evolution and Human Behavior* 30 (2): 85-92. doi:10.1016/j.evolhumbehav.2008.11.001.

Epstein, D. 2014. *The Sports Gene: Inside the Science of Extraordinary Athletic Performance.* Portfolio.

Epstein, R. 2016. *The empty brain.* May 18. https://aeon.co/essays/you r-brain-does-not-process-information-and-it-is-not-a-computer.

Fang, M, and JM Rieger. 2016. *This May Be The Most Horrible Thing That Donald Trump Believes.* Sep 29. https://www.huffpost.com/entry/ donald-trump-eugenics_n_57ec4cc2e4b024a52d2cc7f9.

Fodor, J. 1975. *The Language of Thought.* Crowell.

Frank, R. 2016. *Success and Luck: Good Fortune and the Myth of Meritocracy.* Princeton University Press.

Gallistel, CR, and PD Balsam. 2014. "Time to rethink the neural mechanisms of learning and memory." *Neurobiology of Learning and Memory* 108 (2014) 136–144 141.

Gazzaniga, Michael S. 2011. *Who's in charge? free will and the science of the brain.* New York: Ecco (imprint of HarperCollins).

Gromet, Dena M., Kimberly A. Hartson, and David K. Sherman. 2015. "The politics of luck: Political ideology and the perceived relationship between luck and success." *Journal of Experimental Social Psychology* 59: 40-46.

Haidt, J. 2012. *The righteous mind: Why good people are divided by politics and religion.* New York: Pantheon Books.

Haimovich, G, C Ecker, M Dunagin, and et al. 2017. "Intercellular mRNA trafficking via membrane nanotube-like extensions in mammalian cells." *PNAS* 114 (46) E9873-E9882. doi:10.1073/ pnas.1706365114.

Hameroff, S, and R Penrose. 2013. "Consciousness in the universe: A review of the 'Orch OR' theory." *Physics of Life Reviews.* doi:10.1016/j. plrev.2013.08.002.

Hedman, S (Steffe). n.d. https://schteppe.github.io/p2.js/demos/ragdoll. html.

Holland, J. 2006. "Studying Complex Adaptive Systems." *Journal of Systems Science and Complexity* 19(1): 1-8. http://hdl.handle.net/2027.42/41486.

Hoyle, G, and CA Wiersma. 1977. *Identified neurons and behavior of arthropods.* Plenum Press.

Jarrett, C. 2018. *The bad news on human nature, in 10 findings from psychology.* Dec 5. https://aeon.co/ideas/the-bad-news-on-human-nature-in-10-findings-from-psychology.

Kahn, J. 2012. "Can You Call a 9-Year-Old a Psychopath?" *New York Times.* https://www.nytimes.com/2012/05/13/magazine/can-you-call-a-9-year-old-a-psychopath.html.

Keltner, D, and J Haidt. 2003. "Approaching awe, a moral, spiritual, and aesthetic emotion." *Cognition and Emotion* 59: 17:2, 297-314. doi:10.1080/02699930302297.

Kluger, J. 2006. "How Americans are Living Dangerously." *Time*, Nov 6.

Knight, W. 2016. "An AI with 30 Years' Worth of Knowledge Finally Goes to Work." *MIT Technology Review.* Mar 14. https://www.technologyreview.com/s/600984/an-ai-with-30-years-worth-of-knowledge-finally-goes-to-work/.

Koch, C. 2018. "What Is Consciousness?" *Nature* 557: S8-S12. doi:10.1038/d41586-018-05097-x.

Korb, A. 2015. *The Upward Spiral: Using Neuroscience to Reverse the Course of Depression, One Small Change at a Time.* New Harbinger Publications.

Krizhevsky, A, I Sutskever, and G Hinton. 2017. "ImageNet classification with deep convolutional neural networks." *Communications of the ACM*, June. doi:10.1145/3065386.

Krugman, P. 2019. "Trump Versus the Socialist Menace: The Commies are coming for your pickup trucks." *New York Times*, Feb 7. https://www.nytimes.com/2019/02/07/opinion/trump-socialism-state-of-the-union.html.

Le Bihan, D. 2014. *Looking Inside the Brain: The Power of Neuroimaging.* Princeton University Press.

LeCun, Y, Y Bengio, and G Hinton. 2015. "Deep learning." *Nature* 521 (7553), 436.

Libet, B, C Gleason, E Wright, and D Pearl. 1983. "Time of Conscious Intention to Act in Relation to Onset of Cerebral Activity (Readiness-Potential)." *Brain* 106 (3): 623–42. doi:10.1093/brain/106.3.623. PMID 6640273.

Lieberman, D, and M Long. 2018. *The Molecule of More: How a Single Chemical in Your Brain Drives Love, Sex, and Creativity—and Will Determine the Fate of the Human Race.* BenBella Books.

Loy, J. 2019. *Neural Network Projects with Python: The ultimate guide to using Python to explore the true power of neural networks through six projects.* Packt Publishing. https://towardsdatascience.com/how-to-build-your-own-neural-network-from-scratch-in-python-68998a08e4f6.

Mahler, J. 2015. "The White and Gold (No, Blue and Black!) Dress That Melted the Internet." *New York Times.* https://www.nytimes.com/2015/02/28/business/a-simple-question-about-a-dress-and-the-world-weighs-in.html.

Marcus, G. 2018a. *Deep Learning: A Critical Appraisal.* Jan 2. https://arxiv.org/abs/1801.00631.

—. 2018b. *Innateness, AlphaZero, and Artificial Intelligence.* Jan 17. https://arxiv.org/abs/1801.05667.

Mayford, M, S Siegelbaum, and E Kandel. 2012. "Synapses and Memory Storage." *Cold Spring Harb Perspect Biol.* doi:10.1101/cshperspect.a005751.

McAuliffe, K. 2019. "Liberals and Conservatives React in Wildly Different Ways to Repulsive Pictures." *Atlantic,* Mar. https://www.theatlantic.com/magazine/archive/2019/03/the-yuck-factor/580465/.

Michotte, A. 1946/1963. *The Perception of Causality.* NY: Basic Books (translation).

Mitchell, K. 2018. *Innate: how the wiring of our brains shapes who we are.* Princeton Univ Press.

Moroz, L. 2011. "Aplysia." *Current Biology* 21(2): R60–R61. doi:10.1016/j.cub.2010.11.028.

NIH. 2014. "Hearing Different Frequencies." *NIH.* Jun 2. https://www.nih.gov/news-events/nih-research-matters/ hearing-different-frequencies.

Pinedo, M. 2016. *Scheduling: Theory, Algorithms, and Systems.* Springer.

Pinker, Steven. 1994. *The Language Instinct.* Penguin.

Plutchik, R. 2003. *Emotions and life: Perspectives from psychology, biology, and evolution.* Washington, DC: American Psychological Association.

Popper, Karl. 1959. *The Logic of Scientific Discovery.* Routledge.

Queenan, B. 2017. "On the research of time past: the hunt for the substrate of memory." *Annals of the New York Academy of Sciences* 1396: 108-125. doi:10.1111/nyas.13348.

Quiroga, R Q, L Reddy, G Kreiman, C Koch, and I Fried. 2005. "Invariant visual representation by single neurons in the human brain." *Nature,* Jun: 1102-1107.

Rawls, J. 1971. *A Theory of Justice.* Harvard University Press.

Russell, S, and P Norvig. 2009. *Artificial Intelligence: A Modern Approach (3rd Edition).* Pearson.

Salam, M, and D Victor. 2018. "Yanny or Laurel? How a Sound Clip Divided America." *New York Times.* https://www.nytimes.com/2018/05/15/science/yanny-laurel.html.

Schenk, D. 2011. *The Genius in All of Us: New Insights into Genetics, Talent, and IQ.* Anchor.

Schopenhauer, A. 1839. *On The Freedom Of The Will.* as translated in The Philosophy of American History : The Historical Field Theory (1945) by Morris Zucker, p. 531.

Shomrat, T, and M Levin. 2013. "An automated training paradigm reveals long-term memory in planarians and its persistence through head regeneration." *The Journal of Experimental Biology* 216: 3799-3810. doi:10.1242/jeb.087809.

Smith, A. 1759. *The theory of moral sentiments.* London: Printed for A. Millar, and A. Kincaid and J. Bell.

Snyder, B. 2005. *Save The Cat! The Last Book on Screenwriting You'll Ever Need.* Michael Wiese Productions.

Solem, J E. 2012. *Programming Computer Vision with Python: Tools and algorithms for analyzing images.* O'Reilly Media.

Somers, J. 2017. "Is AI Riding a One-Trick Pony?" *MIT Technology Review*, Nov/Dec.

Sorrells, S, M Paredes, A Cebrian-Silla, and et al. 2018. "Human hippocampal neurogenesis drops sharply in children to undetectable levels in adults." *Nature* 555, pages 377–381. doi:10.1038/nature25975.

Theil, S. 2015. "Why the Human Brain Project Went Wrong—and How to Fix It." *Scientific American.* https://www.scientificamerican.com/article/why-the-human-brain-project-went-wrong-and-how-to-fix-it/.

Thompson, C. 2018. "The Miseducation of Artificial Intelligence." *WIRED*, Dec.

Veve, A. 2018. "Farsighted: Stewart Brand, the man who was wired before WIRED, on the tools he believes will make the whole world better." *WIRED*, Oct.

Wade, N. 2007. *Before the Dawn: Recovering the Lost History of Our Ancestors.* Penguin.

Welch, J, and S Welch. 2006. "It's Not about Empty Suits." *Business Week*, Oct 16.

—. 2008. "Release Your Inner Extrovert." *Business Week*, Nov 26.

Wikipedia. n.d. *The Apprentice.* Mark Barnett. https://en.wikipedia.org/wiki/The_Apprentice_(American_TV_series).

—. n.d. *Wason Selection Task.* https://en.wikipedia.org/wiki/Wason_selection_task.

Yang, A. 2018. *The War on Normal People: the truth about America's disappearing jobs and why universal basic income is our future.* Hachette Books.

ABOUT THE AUTHOR

The author is a computer scientist with a passion for understanding how the mind and brain really work.

CPSIA information can be obtained
at www.ICGtesting.com
Printed in the USA
BVHW071928090819
555523BV00002B/315/P